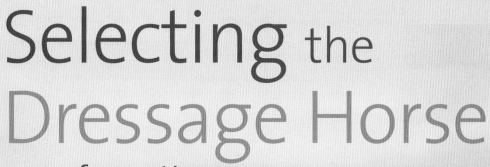

Selecting the Dressage Horse

◎ conformation

◎ movement

◎ temperament

notes and comments by
Anky van Grunsven

Dirk Willem Rosie

Translated by Marji Mc Fadden, M.A.

Trafalgar Square Publishing

copyright

First published in the United States of America in 2006 by
Trafalgar Square Publishing
North Pomfret, Vermont 05053

Printed in China

Originally published in the Dutch language as *Het dressuur paard* by
Fontaine Uitgevers, 's-Graveland, 2005

Copyright © 2005 Fontaine Uitgevers bv, 's-Graveland
English translation © 2006 Trafalgar Square Publishing

Disclaimer of Liability
The author and publisher shall have neither liability nor responsibility to
any person or entity with respect to any loss or damage caused or alleged
to be caused directly or indirectly by the information contained in this
book. While the book is as accurate as the author can make it, there may
be errors, omissions, and inaccuracies.

Library of Congress Cataloging-in-Publication Data

Rosie, Dirk Willem.
 [Dressurpaard. English]
 Selecting the dressage horse : conformation, movement, temperament / Dirk
Willem Rosie ; with commentary by Anky van Grunsven.
     p. cm.
 Includes bibliographical references and index.
 ISBN-13: 978-1-57076-362-5 (hardcover : alk. paper)
 ISBN-10: 1-57076-362-3 (hardcover : alk. paper) 1. Dressage horses. I.
Grunsven, Anky van. II. Title.
 SF309.65R67 2006
 798.2'4--dc22
                    2006027179

Design and typographical editing by x-hoogte, Tilburg; Linda van
Eijndhoven and Hans Lodewijkx

10 9 8 7 6 5 4 3 2 1

Illustration Credits

The photographs in this book were taken mainly by Dirk
Caremans.

Watercolors are by Mary-Ellen Janssen.

The illustrations in chapters 14 and 15 were borrowed
from *Equine Locomotion* by Willem Back and Hilary
Clayton, and were used with permission.

Other Photography
Claartje van Andel (Chapter 17), Animal Sciences Group
Lelystad (Chapter 20), Charlotte Dekker (Chapter 19),
Werner Ernst (Ideaal, Chapter 18), Ton Kruithof
(Montecristo, Chapter 4), KWPN, Sandra Nieuwendijk
(Bragi van Aldenghoor, Chapter 11).

Contents

The KWPN (Royal Dutch Warmblood Studbook) is the Dutch breeding organization for jumping, dressage, carriage, and Gelderlander horses. The KWPN has over 32,000 members in the Netherlands, as well as a North American Department (the NA/WPN), which is now known as the Dutch Warmblood Studbook in North America.

The international success of the Dutch horse is based primarily on performance, durability, and appealing conformation. Each year, an estimated 10,000 new foals are skilfully brought along by some of the world's most modern and successful breeders based on a philosophy that the organization believes will only lead to more success.

A modern association with a rich history, the KWPN remains tied to tradition, but realizes that in this day and age, the Dutch horse is now of completely different value—today, Dutch horses can be found all over the world, often among the top performers in jumping, dressage, and driving competitions. In both 2004 and 2005, the KWPN was ranked first in the world amongst studbooks for its jumping horses, and only the Hanoverian Society was rated above the KWPN for dressage horses.

The KWPN is a network of information and knowledge, but more importantly it is a horse world that bubbles with activity and is run by those devoted to its success.

Preface

Dirk Willem Rosie's presentation during the 2004 Global Dressage Forum in Hooge Mierde, the Netherlands, really captivated me, which was why I was curious about his "dressage book."

The book is fascinating because of its thoroughly scientific approach. The author, known for his critical and expert view on breeding as well as dressage, clearly describes the horse's biomechanics and genetics, as well as temperament and social behavior—all while taking into consideration the horse's nature. In addition, he discusses the horse-and-rider relationship in depth. The enlightening survey of upper level dressage riders and their thoughts on what makes a top dressage horse, and Anky van Grunsven's thoughtful commentary, add further interest and set this book apart.

This book is simply a must-have for anyone who wants a deeper understanding of the dressage horse.

Mariette Withages-Dieltjes
FEI Dressage Committee Chair

October 30, 2004
Schoten, Belgium

7

conformation

1

The Goal of Dressage

Sooner or later, many dressage riders add a dimension to their passion for training and riding horses: competing against others in their sport. The desire to compare their horses' training to others and to do so in front of a judge or panel of judges—a system which is imperfect by definition—is, it would seem, impossible to ignore.

These riders could have stayed home, blissfully training their horses and feeling quite content. Instead they choose to compete, perhaps even becoming frustrated in the process. It is amazing that an activity such as dressage, which is measured subjectively and is, therefore, poorly suited as a system for ranking one above another, has nonetheless developed into an Olympic sport.

The most successful riders in the sport train extremely seriously, and competition ultimately determines who the champion of each country is, and which riders may accompany that champion to the Olympics to compete at Grand Prix level against the best in the world.

Like other Olympic sports, such as figure skating and synchronized swimming, dressage is about achieving a state of physical perfection—developing grace and harmony in a moving body to its full capacity. And, as with so many other sports, the body's balance is an issue. Balance must be maintained through a series of extremely challenging athletic efforts, which sometimes push the body to the edge.

The Horse as a Performer

There is, however, one distinct difference between dressage and Olympic sports that do not involve horses: it is not the human athlete's body that, through training, grows closer to perfection but that of the athlete's horse. A competent judge will score a dressage rider by his horse's performance, with the exception of penalties for a rider whose legs are not quiet or whose seat is crooked. And yet, it is the rider, not the horse, who receives the medal!

If, in fact, the horse—and not the rider—is the athlete, then why isn't dog agility (for example) an Olympic sport, as well? Both dog and horse are wonders of domestication that have flourished alongside man for thousands of years; however, because of the necessary physical and mental unity between horse and rider, the horse has developed into a different sort of sporting companion to the human athlete—and therefore an athlete in his own right. A dog is trained by commands given at a distance, but a horse "operates" in a very physical way with someone sitting on his back, forming a partnership with the human who intuitively reads his body and corrects his balance and movement with alternative aids when necessary.

The Regulations

In contrast to dog agility, dressage is not really about obedience—although it is always fascinating to see a powerful, 1300-pound creature completely submissive to the requests of a petite, 100-pound woman (as is often the case).

At this point, we should establish that dressage,

thankfully, is not primarily about obedience but about realizing a horse's potential for movement. The Fédération Equestre Internationale (FEI) is the international organization that determines the contents of the dressage rulebook. For a long time, the *FEI Rulebook* stated that "the harmonious development of the organism and of the horse's natural qualities" was the goal of the sport. In 2004, the goal was revised to advocate "the development of the horse into a happy athlete through harmonious education." We now know that the way a horse moves, in particular, appears to be crucial to that idea of "harmonious education." Therefore, the quality of a horse's gaits is a key consideration, as well as the ease and naturalness with which a horse performs required movements.

Further, the *FEI Rulebook* states the following:
"The horse thus gives the impression of doing of his own accord what is required of him. Confident and attentive, he submits generously to the control of his rider..."

Both grace and harmony play a part in a horse's movement and the ease with which he performs dressage exercises. Watching a dressage test is an aesthetic experience, emphasizing the beauty of horse and rider synchronicity.

Obedience

In competitive dressage, "obedience" is expected from both horse and rider. If a rider fails to make a transition at the required letter, his score is justifiably lowered. However, in ascertaining a prospective dressage horse's capabilities, a rider first considers the horse's movement, and then later deals with obedience and other invisible qualities, such as the desire to perform, perseverance, and the ability to work through fatigue—and perhaps even pain—if necessary. We will discuss the horse's temperament in depth later in this book, but ultimately, the sport of dressage is about competition and those qualities that are visible: the physical appearance of a graceful horse and rider team, radiating power, suppleness, rhythm, and regularity of strides.

It is fascinating to see a powerful 1300-pound creature completely submissive to the will of a petite woman, as seen here with Corlandus and Margit Otto-Crépin.

Man and Horse

The horse and rider partnership is like a dance, with man clearly in the leading position. He uses subtle aids to tell his horse to perform a movement or shorten or lengthen stride. In a training program spanning many years, he makes his partner strong, patiently teaching his horse all the required steps, and schooling and gymnasticizing him to a very high level.

When horse and rider unite, a dynamic relationship forms that is often not apparent to onlookers. Horse and rider give each other physical and mental signals, and then—when all goes well—mutually respond to those signals. It is a fascinating process of "on-line" communication between two bodies and two spirits. What goes on between the mind and the body of the horse? How does he deal with the work, which is sometimes extremely demanding? Does he take any

ment. These three components, combined and inextricably bound together, are molded, like clay, in the hands of the rider or trainer.

While the horse's physical performance wins or loses a class, the rider—not the horse—determines the pair's path and eventual destination. The rider selects a horse to train in dressage and begins the journey, intent on discovering the depth of his horse's latent talents. Whether or not the horse can actually achieve a state of physical perfection is based on this potential ability and how much time his rider can devote to the pursuit of the team's goals.

"Does a horse feel 'happy' when he wins a class?" asks Anky. "I don't believe horses' minds work like that, except for Bonnie [Bonfire], of course. In Sydney, I am sure he knew we had won."

pleasure in the horse and rider harmony that so pleases his human partner, or is he simply submitting to the rider's will because the rider is in the dominant position until he can return to his stall?

A Living Instrument

Man and horse: a *pas de deux* of lead dancer and prima ballerina. Each has his own leading role, yet it is *the horse* that makes the difference between mediocre performance and brilliance. The horse's body expresses every movement by way of the rider's direction, and the rider is judged time and again on the quality of his horse and, most importantly, how he exhibits that quality.

Compared to other equestrian disciplines, the dressage horse holds a unique position as a living "sports instrument." The horse's body in motion directly determines the outcome of a competition, not a stopwatch or a knocked-down jump rail. In dressage, the Olympic gold medal can be lost if a horse's hind leg is not off the ground quickly enough or if his body swings slightly back and forth during flying changes. For this reason, a horse's potential usefulness as a top dressage prospect depends entirely on his conformation, movement, and tempera-

The outcome of a dressage competition is directly determined by the horse's moving body, rather than a stopwatch or a knocked-down jump rail.

ANKY VAN GRUNSVEN

Submission?

As stated in this chapter, the dressage horse is indeed your "sports instrument" from the moment you start riding him, but that's true of other horses, too. A horse must simply be suited to whichever discipline his rider chooses to pursue.

Let's talk about this idea of the horse as an "instrument." If you play an instrument, then you make beautiful, or sometimes ugly, sounds. Therefore, if the horse is an instrument, the rider has the responsibility to make beautiful or ugly sounds. (When I think of an instrument, however, I think of an object, and a horse, for me, is anything but an object!)

As far as I'm concerned, a dressage horse does not have to be physically beautiful; however, he should evoke emotion or a sense of beauty by the way he moves. There are many horses that meet the various standards for a dressage horse, but when you see them go, they just don't give you that certain "feeling"—and that's exactly what I look for.

It's like this: a good judge gives the horse a score for the way he performs a dressage test. However, a nice horse could receive a poor score due to his rider's lack of skill because a bad rider is unable to truly showcase his horse's talents. You don't see the horse performing alone—although if the riding is very good, then in a way you, the judge, and the rest of the audience, *only* see the horse.

This is one reason why I continue to be a supporter of the dressage uniform—the coat and hat—because the picture of the rider should be *constant*, not distracting. If you know exactly what a rider did during a test—every aid that she gave—then that rider was a distraction. The eye should always be drawn to the horse, *not* the rider.

The word *submission* is often used when discussing dressage and I think that's wrong. I don't want to deal with my horses in this way. A horse that submits to his rider loses his personality. What's nice about dressage is that it actually amplifies a horse's personality. If you're a good rider, then it's really fun to enter the arena with a horse that's a bit of a character. The very art of dressage is not forcing your horse into submission but rather making him obedient by focusing his attention on you. If you work very consistently at home, rewarding the right things and correcting the wrong things every day, then eventually your horse will know what he's doing, and while I don't think every horse necessarily enjoys doing Grand Prix dressage, I do think that real sport horses can perform their work with great satisfaction.

I don't think horses feel "happy" if they win a class. I don't believe their minds work like that—except for Bonnie [Bonfire], of course. In Sydney, I am sure he knew that we had won.

13

2 Jumpers versus Dressage Horses

There are many horses that can never achieve the physical perfection required of an Olympic dressage champion. Such horses far outnumber those that can cope with the physical and mental demands of the sport at its highest level. It is logical that millions of horses will never win the Olympic gold medal in dressage simply because their conformation prevents them from doing so: their legs are short and placed too far under their bodies; their neck is short and low-set; or their croup is four inches higher than their withers. Horse training has advanced considerably in 6,000 years, but we still cannot achieve the impossible!

People can certainly agree about such extreme conformation flaws as I've mentioned above; however, a great deal of confusion surrounds other aspects of the ideal dressage horse's build. People offer Anky van Grunsven's Bonfire and Isabell Werth's Gigolo as examples that conformation is, in fact, unimportant to a dressage horse's success. "If these two horses could determine the image of world-class dressage for years, then there is no point in discussing the 'ideal' conformation of a dressage horse," reason some trainers. Not only is it thought that Bonfire and Gigolo lacked physical beauty, but trainers also point out the significant conformational differences between the two former international competitors.

Breeders versus Trainers/Riders

It is quite interesting that trainers and riders often reason this way—despite not having specific interest in or particular knowledge of breeding. As breeders, we do not fault them for paying little attention to the things that are common knowledge for us, such as functional conformation, bloodlines, and hereditary ability. As long as breeders and trainers/riders maintain a dialogue, it is better that each fulfils their own role. What is cause for concern are the differences between the groups' viewpoints. The quote above dismissing the importance of conformation because Bonfire and Gigolo are so unalike overlooks the fact that the two horses—although very different in size, presence, and movement—share several functional qualities of a dressage horse: a rectangular body shape, long legs, a well-placed neck with sufficient length, and good muscling.

It is certainly worth noting that riders' and trainers' views stem from their own attitudes and experiences; lessons they've learned and their desire to improve on what they've learned and not repeat past mistakes. The rider views *the horse* as a constant, reasoning from the saddle: "I'm sitting here. Now, what can I do to improve my results?" On the other hand, breeders consider a horse very critically, viewing *the rider* as a constant. Thus, each takes his position.

Although admittedly breeders and riders don't always completely understand one another, they certainly have each other's interests at heart.

The Ideal Conformation

Because trainers and riders may have a different understanding of conformation than breeders, we will discuss the "ideal" build for a dressage horse extensively later in this book.

"If Bonfire and Gigolo [with their significant physical differences] could determine the image of world-class dressage for years, then there is no point in discussing the 'ideal' conformation of a dressage horse," reason some trainers.

Different opinions also exist among breeders. The concept of "ideal" is rather subjective; therefore, let us first establish *whose* ideal we are discussing: the Royal Warmblood Studbook of the Netherlands, or KWPN (represented in the US by the Dutch Warmblood Studbook in North America, or NA/WPN). The studbook ideal is based on a combination of physics, science, and practical experience. Logic and practice together make a reliable compass.

Now, before we go further let us briefly mention the man responsible for the concept i*deal.* The Greek philosopher Plato described the human understanding of "ideal" as shadows cast by light. We can strive to see the "light," but in the end our limited world of human perception forces us to make do with the shadow. This concept can be applied to the world of horses. We use the ideal as a compass to direct our path, but do we

actually achieve perfection?

In the pages to come, we will discuss the ideal conformation of a dressage horse based on the science of physics and the preference of top dressage riders. This does not suggest that horses are automatically successful if they meet this ideal construction, nor does it mean that horses cannot be successful if they do not meet the ideal in all respects. After all, there are other necessary considerations, such as temperament and the desire to perform, and one of the things that breeders need to learn from riders is that they still do not pay enough attention to qualities not visible to the eye. Laziness or an inclination to be uncooperative are not immediately apparent; however, a rider will be confronted with these issues during training and may find himself sitting on a beautiful horse—with "ideal" conformation—that shuts down completely when he really has to work.

15

Jumpers and dressage horses are similar in many ways, and vastly different in others. Anky van Grunsven's Gestion Salinero and Korean jumper rider Jung-Ho Woo's Seven Up both participated in the Olympic games in Athens. Salinero and his rider won the individual gold medal in dressage, while Seven Up helped rank Korea in ninth place in team jumping. Salinero and Seven Up are full brothers, by the stallion Salieri out of a dam by Lungau, and bred in Hannover, Germany.

Functional Conformation

The ideal *conformation* of a dressage horse is functional conformation: the build best suited for the discipline for which the horse is used. In the 1980s, when Dutch horse breeders had intense discussions concerning breeding beautiful horses versus breeding horses specifically for sport, the late Gert van der Veen, Chief Inspector of the KWPN, asserted that "beauty is as beauty does," thus explaining the phenomena of horses such as Bonfire and Gigolo that are not particularly attractive in their stalls but can captivate the whole world when performing.

Like many other types of horses, the body of the dressage horse directly determines his suitability for dressage work. Two other examples include the draft horse, which has become short-legged and heavy through centuries of selective breeding, and the Thoroughbred, which was bred to become long-legged and lightweight. In contrast to the generations that have been spent perfecting draft horses and Thoroughbreds, selectively breeding Warmbloods for specific qualities is still in its infancy. Because jumping and dressage—in many regards the two most important disciplines in equestrian sports—are totally different disciplines, we can obviously conclude that over time, jumpers and dressage horses will become clearly different from each other with distinct discipline-specific conformational and

ANKY VAN GRUNSVEN

Chance Hits

If you compare Gigolo's conformation to Bonfire's, you can certainly find similarities. For me, however, the "feeling" you get from a horse is the deciding factor, and in that respect, I see big differences between the two horses in terms of both presence and movement. Gigolo is more of a worker, while Bonfire moves gracefully. When Gigolo comes to mind, I think of athletics; and when I consider Bonfire, I think of ballet.

It's easy to say, "A horse with long front legs scores higher than a comparably trained horse with short and/or front legs that are 'camped under.'" However, in practice, you never see horses that are identical in every way except for the length of their front legs. (In general, I do feel that a dressage horse with long front legs is visually more appealing than one with short front legs.)

I think my horses are absolutely wonderful, and if there's a mistake, then it's because I did something wrong. Maybe only once a year will I come out of the arena and think, "I really rode well." But even then I can't think about it too long or I'll find some flaw. Riders are very self-critical—and breeders are, too. Despite this, and other similarities, when I see what breeders produce, I can't say I always understand the line of thinking—although I do sometimes get it. For example, there was a lot of criticism regarding using Cocktail, one of my Grand Prix horses, as a breeding stallion. His back was a bit hollow, and I certainly know

that his canter could have been better, but that horse had so many strong points—characteristics that were far more important than his weak points. If I consider how many good dressage horses Cocktail produced, given that he sired relatively few horses, then I think Cocktail was an incredibly good breeding stallion, in spite of his hollow back and weak canter.

Breeders are more and more on the rider's side because they now understand that stallions that perform well produce offspring that perform well, which is why it's important that stallions participate in competitive dressage. A stallion that competes and proves himself demonstrates that he is mentally and physically suited for the job, and so it is more likely the foals he parents will be suited as well.

I know several stallions quite well because I've ridden them, and I see a lot of their traits in their offspring. What do I notice the most? Temperament. When I was in Zwolle, the Netherlands, for TCN Partout's farewell in 2003, I saw a number of his offspring perform and thought that I'd certainly like to have them in my barn, too!

I agree that there are, in fact, many commonalities between jumpers and dressage horses. My horse Salinero, for example, was actually bred for jumping, and his full brother is a Grand Prix jumper. Based on that, it seems that top horses from different disciplines are simply chance hits.

temperamental qualities. A further "conformational separation" of the subpopulation of top jumpers and dressage horses from the present general population of riding horses is indeed unavoidable, primarily because of the very specific requirements for the sport of dressage and of dressage horses.

We should not forget that in addition to the clear differences between different types of riding horses, important similarities exist. These similarities are evident in the fact that jumping and dressage riders share the same general requirements for the way their horses "work," mechanically speaking. For example, they want to sit in the middle of the horse, with just as much forehand in front of them as hindquarters behind them. This is why breeders impose the general requirement of a 1: 1: 1 ratio between the forehand, barrel, and hindquarters, because the development and placement of the withers and the shoulder play a very important part with respect to positioning the rider in the middle of the horse.

Another important requirement concerns body size: the horse should not be too big, too small, too fine, or too coarse. Both jumper and dressage riders value "rideability" in a horse; in other words, a horse that works without requiring excessive physical effort from the rider. For this reason, we pay considerable attention to a fine head-neck connection and sufficient neck length. Durability is another requirement that the horse's body must meet, which is why selection inspectors always stress the importance of a correctly built animal. In addition, there are per-sonality qualities commonly desired for jumping and dressage horses: enthusiasm, desire to work, and reliability are valued by all riders. (Although temperament characteristics were named last, they are certainly not the least important. We will discuss all these topics in detail later in this book. I mention them now to emphasize the similarities between jumpers and dressage horses.)

One significant difference between horses bred for dressage and those for jumping or eventing is that a dressage horse's competitive ability is directly affected by his conformation to a far greater degree than jumpers or eventers. For example, a horse with long front legs generally scores higher than a comparably trained horse with short and/or front legs that are "camped under."

We must consider one more component in breeding horses with ideal conformation based on functional qualities specifically for dressage: consideration for the animal itself—as Gert van der Veen (mentioned earlier in this book) always pointed out. Van der Veen asserted that horses find joy in life mainly in physical ways. A good conversation or a twenty-five-year marriage doesn't make them happy; good feed and good care does. It is important to allow horses to have a social life in a pasture and train them for work that they can easily perform. I feel it is the solemn duty of breeders to gauge whether they are delivering horses that are physically capable of performing dressage movements over many years without having to endure debilitating mental stress.

The "Uphill" Horse

There is a great deal of difference between evaluating the conformation of sport horses and the conformation of, say, West Highland Terriers or Persian cats. There is no breed description, no prescribed color, no requirements for how the ears should curl—only the horse's function in sport, which in this case is dressage. The FEI creates the required tests, and the dressage horse breeder responds.

Horse breeders are market-oriented. They do their best to meet the demands of dressage riders all over the world. And those riders, in turn, have a list of requirements obtained from the *FEI Rulebook*. So, if the world equestrian sports federation and the affiliated national associations decided to replace the extended trot with the tölt, then a number of well-developed Icelandic horses would undoubtedly turn up at the next stallion selection.

When considering the dressage horse's function, we cannot avoid studying the Grand Prix movement specifications. The theme of the entire sport of dressage—from the national levels on up—is continuous preparation for the most difficult tests. At the end of the training process, dressage is about extreme degrees of collection combined with fluent transitions to extended gaits, among other things, and the horse must not only have command of both the piaffe and extended trot, but also be able to interweave these exercises harmoniously. The same applies to the pirouette and the extended canter.

The required extremes in trot and canter are very clear examples of exercises that are directly related to an "uphill" body and neck. However, a horse can also perform the lateral movements better if he is built uphill. Balance and rhythm, for example, are achieved through lightening the forehand by shifting the horse's weight to his hindquarters. Horses should move in this elevated way so they can perform a half-pass with precisely the same rhythm and regularity with which they move straight ahead.

FEI rules explicitly discuss the type of movement that is geared toward performing the collected exercises, and that movement is directly related to conformation. Article 401, paragraph 2.3 discusses the "lightness of the forehand and the engagement of the hindquarters."

It should be emphasized again that fluent transitions from the utmost collection to the greatest extension can only be achieved after years of professional training; however, an uphill horse is necessary from the beginning for correct collection, transitions, and lateral movements.

Weight Distribution

We use the concept "uphill" as the opposite of "downhill." The expression "uphill" precisely describes the direction of the dressage horse's development. A horse that is built "downhill" moves with too much weight placed on the forehand, resulting in a "downhill way of going"—something that we all have seen. A naturally uphill horse is conformationally less inclined to place too much weight on the forehand; as a result, the uphill horse is better equipped to move with his weight evenly distributed over four legs.

Additional parts of the horse's body are affected by an uphill build, in particular, the front legs and the neck. To get an idea of the extent to which a horse is built

Even a fabulous rider like Tineke Bartels, pictured here on the long-legged Broere Jazz, cannot change a naturally short-strided Przewalski horse into a big-moving dressage horse.

uphill, we need to look at the complete horse, not just his parts. It is only then we can see if the withers is at least as high as the croup, and if the forehand naturally "arches upward" relative to the rest of the horse.

Long-Legged

A dressage horse should have long legs. The term "high-legged" has long had a negative connotation among breeders, suggesting a horse of insufficient size and flank depth, a wasp-waisted creature without well-sprung ribs—in short, a horse that is not "well-bred." Now, though, "high-legged" may be in reference to the length of limb rather than a lack of depth in the body. And while everything must be in proportion, long legs are part of a dressage horse's *correct* proportions.

ANKY VAN GRUNSVEN

Self-Carriage

Breeders certainly have to serve a specific market, but I don't think we have to be *too* concerned about the possibility of the extended trot being replaced by the tölt! In the case of dressage horse breeders, let me be very clear: we shouldn't make any concessions in terms of the most important aspects of a dressage horse, such as conformational correctness. Years ago, I participated in performance testing at stallion evaluations. I remember thinking it was very strange that a stallion with weak hind end movement was approved. A breed or a studbook represents something—in the case of the KWPN, it represents the sport horse, so the horse *must* meet the requirements for the sport.

To be honest, I don't consider my Spanish colleagues' Andalusians to be true sport horses. I enjoy seeing them perform the collected exercises in demonstrations, like the Lipazzaners at the Spanish Riding School in Vienna, because they naturally have a lot of talent for collection. But, collection alone doesn't make a sport horse, and sometimes I don't understand why they earn high scores on certain parts of a test.

As a rider, I'm intensely involved with my horses, but I don't really pay much attention to their conformation. Now, when I read about the "uphill" horse, I can say I recognize it is an important aspect of a dressage horse's conformation, but as a competitive rider, I focus on other things—in addition to my horse's conformation.

The previous chapter mentioned Gert van der Veen. He always said that a horse can enjoy his work more if he has been bred to do his work easily. I completely agree with that statement. However, I don't believe that an uphill conformation is the first priority for a horse to enjoy dressage work. After all, what's the benefit of good self-carriage if the horse is slow with his hind legs?

Self-carriage, of course, is part of the ideal, but self-carriage must function in movement. If a young horse moves correctly but isn't yet able to carry himself, then I can develop the horse's self-carriage through training. I'd rather make concessions when it comes to a horse's conformation than compromise good movement.

21

The pirouette (demonstrated in the top photo by Marlies van Baalen on Blom's Idocus) and the extended canter (bottom photo: Isabell Werth on Anthony) are the opposite ends of the canter scale. Training a horse to perform both these exercises is easier if the horse is built "uphill."

Breeders have enormous power to mold Mother Nature. Consider the huge number of dog breeds that have appeared in "only" 500 years of selective breeding.

Look at the impressive increase in milk production by dairy cows in twenty-five years. We can thank a similar quirk of nature for being able to breed horses like Bonfire and Broere Jazz from the original horse, which differed little physically from the Przewalski horse of today. Long-legged athletes are able to vary their stride length because of their long limbs. Even great riders like Anky van Grunsven and Tineke Bartels cannot change a short-strided Przewalski horse into a big-moving dressage horse.

Paragraph 8 of Article 401 of the *FEI Rulebook* states: *"'The rhythm that a horse maintains in all his paces is fundamental to Dressage."*

If the horse must maintain his rhythm and is required to perform collected as well as extended walk, trot, and canter, then he must be physically able to vary his stride length. It is logical that long legs, which "swing" back and forth, have a greater maximum reach than short legs and therefore can meet the requirements of stride variation more easily. Long legs can make bigger strides; however, the *duration* of a single stride is not affected by the length of the legs: a horse with short legs is, in theory, just as able to vary the duration of his stride as a long-legged horse; his strides are just shorter, which some judges perceive as a difference in quality.

In practice, FEI judges have difficulty scoring these types of quality differences. Andalusian horses, for example, are exceptionally well received in Grand Prix level dressage, although they are usually stocky, short-legged animals with average basic gaits, and they tend to show little bend in the lateral movements.

The Importance of Long Front Legs 4

We concluded in the previous chapter that a dressage horse should have long legs, and we assess this athletic quality relative to the whole horse. There is another reason to strive for long front legs: to a large extent, the front limbs determine the placement of the *axis*—the imaginary horizontal line running from the hindquarters to the chest through the middle of the horse's barrel. If this line slopes downward from the hindquarters to the forehand, then the horse is built "downhill."

A horse's head and neck move considerably more than the tail. As a result, approximately 60 percent of the horse's weight *naturally* rests on the forehand. If we add a downward-sloping axis to this equation, it is easy to predict what will happen when the horse moves. Forward movement combined with the downhill build pushes the horse's mass onto the forehand, which gets heavy and low while the hindquarters get light and high—exactly the *opposite* process of that which is central to all dressage training. Even a very good trainer will—literally—have his hands full when attempting to lighten the forehand of this type of horse.

The conclusions reached in the previous chapter were important, and therefore, I'll repeat them: an elevated forehand is the foundation for collection; moreover, a direct correlation exists between an elevated forehand and carrying power in movement, which enables a horse to move with rhythmic purity. (Ultimately, an elevated forehand is not the only factor affecting carrying power and collection. In the course

of this book, we will also extensively discuss the use of the hind legs.) The Linear Score Sheet used at the KWPN inspections reveals the importance attached to an elevated forehand. This Linear Score Sheet is used to evaluate conformational aspects of the horse, such as neck position and gait quality.

Front Leg Position

The desired length of the front legs—and the related elevation of the forehand—is not just a matter of inches. The *position* of the front legs also influences their length and their athletic use. When looking at the front legs, we may think of the shoulder and the barely visible humerus as part of the body, but mechanically speaking, these parts are completely integrated with the point of the elbow, radius and ulna, knee, cannon bone, pastern joint, pastern, and hoof—in short, the readily visible lower parts of the front limbs. With the slightest flexion of heavily muscled shoulder and a small opening of the angle between the shoulder and humerus, the underlying—and much lighter—parts of the front limbs reach forward with length and elasticity. In order for this mechanism to work smoothly, allowing the horse to vary his stride from short and collected to long and extended, the shoulder must have ample length and sufficient slope. (We use the term "sufficiently sloped" for good reason.) Scientific research has yet to show a connection between a sloping shoulder and dressage performance; however, if we view the shoulder from a strictly mechanical perspective, a long, sloping shoulder allows greater range of motion for the front legs than does a short, straight shoulder.

In the book *Equine Locomotion* (W.B. Saunders Company, 2000), Hilary Clayton, BVMS, Ph.D., MRCVS, of Michigan State University and Wim Back, DVM, Ph.D., Dipl. ECVS, Dipl. RNVA, of Utrecht University in the Netherlands assert that the primary importance of a sloping shoulder relates to proper saddle placement. A long, sloping shoulder places the saddle in the middle of the horse, thus preventing too much of the rider's weight from resting on the forehand. The rider has just as much horse in front of him as behind him—the ideal position to work with his "partner in motion." In addition, this position allows the horse's front legs complete freedom of movement.

Horses with short, straight shoulders need a foregirth to prevent the rider's weight from resting too much on the horse's forehand. Breeders intend to make the foregirth (which was more common in the past than now) unnecessary.

The Shoulder Joint

There is a third, very important aspect of the shoulder as part of the front limb. The position of the shoulder determines the invisible angle formed by the humerus and the scapula and, therefore, influences the position of the entire front leg. This angle should be a minimum of 90 degrees. A too-small angle between the scapula and the humerus caused by a too-sloped shoulder and humerus results in a "camped under" horse—a horse with front limbs placed too far under his body. Furthermore, small angles often translate into shorter front legs. Front legs that are placed too far under the body and/or camped under legs clearly mechanically hinder a horse from moving with long, expressive strides.

A Long Humerus

In the 1990s, the Swedish biomechanics expert Mikael Holmström compared a group of elite dressage horses with a group of average horses. He asserted, among other things, that a good dressage horse clearly has a longer humerus than an average horse. This is quite

logical if you think about it: a long humerus means a longer triceps muscle that facilitates the elbow's movement. The elbow joint is vital to front leg function, which we will discuss later.

Holmström's study showed a greater and clearer positive correlation between a long humerus and dressage ability than between a long radius and dressage ability, which is remarkable, considering the old equine rule of thumb that a horse should have a long radius and a short front cannon.

Durability

Breeders and judges give special consideration to the correct distribution of the downward forces affecting the moving horse's front legs. This may be assessed by viewing a horse from the side and drawing an imaginary line down through the radius, knee, and front cannon. The line should be unbroken by the knee—the midpoint. If the knee protrudes in front of the line, then the horse is "over at the knee"; if it falls behind the line, the horse is "back at the knee." Both cases result in extra stress on the limbs, with risk increasing the greater the deviation from the straight line.

The angle of the pastern and the heel of the foot are responsible, to a great extent, for the correct processing of downward forces. An unbroken imaginary line should also run through the pastern and the hoof. The angle between the foot axis and the ground should not be less than 45 degrees (sloping pasterns) and not greater than 50 degrees (straight pasterns). A so-called "broken hoof axis," caused by a high heel and a weak pastern, results in an unequal distribution of forces. Hoof shape processes downward forces, as well. The hoof must be sufficiently broad—a well-developed foot has a greater contact surface with the ground.

"Stance of Pasterns," "Shape of Feet," and "Heels" appear as separate points on the KWPN (and NA/WPN) Linear Score Sheet used at all studbook inspections.

Suspension

If we only consider durability, then we do the pastern

joint a disservice. The horse occupies a unique position in the animal kingdom as a result of the remarkable spring action of the pasterns. A dressage horse owes a great deal of his "dance talent" to his pastern joints. The pastern area functions as a temporary depot for *kinetic energy* (I expand upon this in my discussion in chapter 15—see p. 77). The tendons, rather than the pastern bones, are actually responsible for temporarily storing energy. Bones cannot expand and contract, but tendons can. I return to Holmström who, during his study in the 1990s, also compared the pastern length of top dressage horses and jumpers with that of average horses. The top horses had longer pasterns, but the angle they formed with the ground did not differ from that of the average horses.

A horse's conformation should be assessed for durability from the front and the rear, as well as from the side. An obvious "toe-in" stance, in which the toes point toward one another, or "toe-out" stance, where the toes clearly point away from one another, not only cause extra stress on the limbs, but are also often coupled with "plaiting" (where the striding leg crosses in front of the supporting leg in a way similar to a person walking a tight rope) or "paddling" (an outward deviation of the foot during flight), gait defects that judges dislike.

With respect to front leg stress, horses with a slight toe-out stance suffer from fewer stress-related problems than horses with a toe-in stance. This is because the horse's center of gravity has an asymmetrical effect on processing downward forces: the insides of the hooves are closer to the horse's center of gravity and so are subject to higher levels of stress. A slightly toe-out stance serves to counterbalance this asymmetry.

Stride Completion

The length and position of the front legs not only affect a horse's conformation but also his way of moving, and particularly the way he completes his strides. We have all seen a "choppy" mover—a horse that cannot move elegantly and expressively because his legs are placed too far under his body and/or are too short.

Long front legs, naturally placed at the very front of the horse's barrel, are just one aspect of the uphill horse. The other aspect is the neck. Together, these two form the forehand, the most prevalent characteristic by which the modern dressage horse is now recognized and judged.

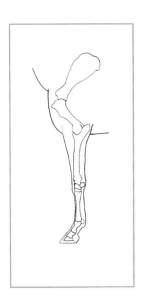

This illustration depicts the important parts of the front leg that are not visible to the eye (left).

The KWPN stallion Montecristo's desirable uphill build is due to more than just his long front legs (right).

ANKY VAN GRUNSVEN

Use of the Shoulders and Knees

This shouldn't surprise anyone: I really don't look at the way the front legs are placed when the horse is standing still. I think the most important question is, "How do those front legs move?" I like to see a horse move with freedom in his shoulder and a bit of knee action, so the movement should really come from both the shoulder and the knee.

Sjef and I always pay attention to the length of the radius: the part of the front legs between the shoulder and the knee should be long enough to function well. I used to think that a horse had to be built quite broad in order to use his front legs well. (That was during the era of Bo and Cocktail.) However, Bonfire, and especially Gestion Krack C, aren't built that wide but use their front legs perfectly, just as I like.

It is certainly important that a horse stands straight on his legs—but more important that a horse *moves* nice and straight. Kir Royal's front legs weren't really that great, but it was hardly noticeable when he moved. And it should be remembered that a young horse may be a bit crooked due to instability. Once the horse gets stronger and develops better balance in his movement, the crookedness often disappears.

A horse's feet are extremely important, but that responsibility belongs to my farrier, Rob Renirie. He always says, "You can't get to the top without Rob." I don't argue with him!

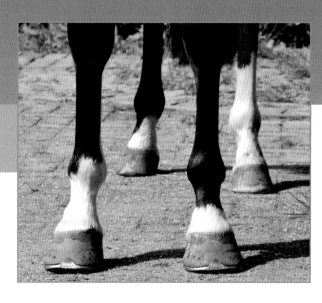

This horse would be marked as having a slighty toed-out stance on the KWPN (NA/WPN) Linear Score Sheet.

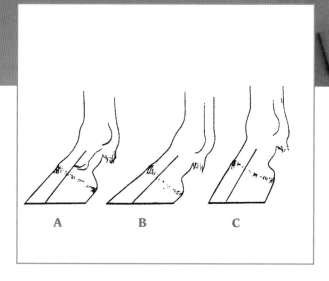

A. Correct pasterns and well-developed heels
B. Long sloping pasterns and low heels
C. Straight pasterns and high heels

The Neck: An Excellent Instrument 5

The horse's neck seems to be full of contradictions. It is responsible for the horse carrying 60 percent of his weight on the forehand—a disadvantageous distribution of weight. However, if the neck is well built, then it is an excellent instrument for riding a horse well. The modern dressage horse is distinguished by his neck!

Dressage riders begin at a disadvantage because horses carry more weight on their forehands than on their hindquarters. This ratio—60 percent on the forehand and 40 percent on the hindquarters—must be gradually shifted through training to eventually become an equal distribution of weight. In order to accomplish this shift, the hind legs must be activated in movement and correct contact—acceptance of the bit—must be achieved.

The neck is decidedly important for this contact. When we consider the concept of contact, we normally associate it with the horse's mouth. However, as a physical component of the horse's body, the mouth, strictly speaking, is hardly relevant. The mouths of all horses, in theory, are sensitive enough to accept a bit without tension. The determining factor is the quality of the connection between the horse and rider: the quiet communication between hand and mouth, the maneuverability of the pivot mechanism of the horse's poll, and the ability of the neck to flex, and shorten and lengthen. These are all aspects directly connected to the neck conformation.

In **Article 401, paragraph 6**, the *FEI Rulebook* states the following regarding contact and the neck:

"A horse is said to be 'on the bit' when the neck is more or less raised and arched according to the stage of training and the extension or collection of the pace.... The head should remain in a steady position, as a rule slightly in front of the vertical, with a supple poll as the highest point of the neck."

Contact

The neck's functionality is evaluated by at least four characteristics on the KWPN (NA/WPN) Linear Score Sheet that was cited in chapter 4. These include "Head-Neck Connection," "Length of Neck," "Position of Neck," and "Muscling of Neck." All these characteristics affect the degree to which a rider can influence the front end of the horse. The process of the horse seeking the contact is easier and smoother if the horse has a "light" (clean) head-neck connection, and a neck of good length that naturally arches upward.

Let's discuss that very important head-neck connection. The highest line of the neck should be a good hand's width behind the horse's ears so he has the physical space to flex at the poll. The poll—the first vertebrae or the *atlas*—should be the highest point. If the highest point is further down the neck, as is the case with some Arabians, it allows the horse to easily curl behind the bit and avoid contact. The head-neck connection also has an underside: the jowls and the throatlatch. Problems with contact, as well as other training problems, frequently stem from heavy jowls and a thick throatlatch because they prevent the horse from flexing comfortably. Therefore, a dressage horse should have a "light," clean, refined throatlatch area connecting the head and neck.

A horse with a long neck is better equipped to perform when his carriage is altered by contact than one with a short neck. (This desired characteristic is related to the length of the horse's entire body and will be discussed later.) When ridden with contact, the horse's frame gets shorter and acquires an elastic tension as a result of accepting the contact and activating his hindquarters. This is due to the combined action of the muscle groups the horse uses to flex from hocks to poll. The length of the neck, in part, makes the front end of this athletic flexion possible.

Neck Position

A refined head-neck connection and a long neck are essential, but the neck's *position* on the horse's body is possibly even *more* essential. A dressage horse distinguishes himself from other riding horses by the position of his neck because he (more so than other riding horses) must move with an elevated forehand.

A horse's neck should naturally arch upward from the horse's body, and not because the horse is raising his head! This kind of neck is easily carried by the horse; on the other hand, a horizontally positioned neck (one that extends out from the body in a flat line rather than curving upward) has to be "lifted," so to speak—to the detriment of the necessary connection over the topline. If you view the horse in a natural stance from the side, you should be able to draw an imaginary line along the middle of the neck from the body to the head. The line should run upward in a slanted, flowing line. There is a trick to check this: look at the topline of the neck (particularly the connection with the withers) and the underside of the neck, starting at the chest. If these two lines and the imaginary line through the middle of the neck create the impression the neck is set a few inches lower than the horse's body, then the horse is "ewe-necked." This flaw physically hinders a horse from being ridden with an elevated forehand.

The bones of the neck do not actually follow the topline of the neck, but rather the line from the middle of the chest, at the height of the point of the shoulder, to the poll.

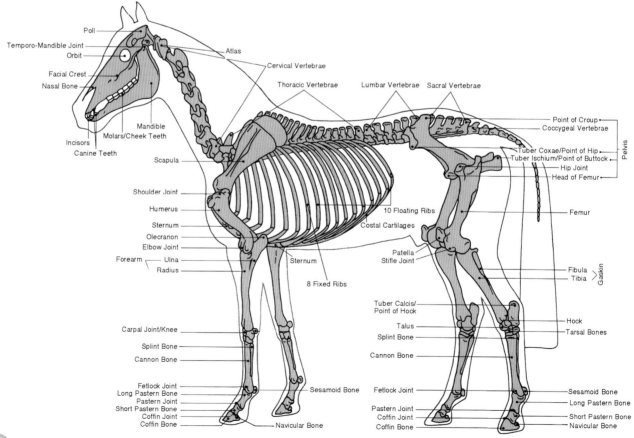

This horse, bred for jumping, has a horizontally positioned neck. It extends from the body in a line that is flat rather than curving upward.

The same applies to the horizontally positioned neck I mentioned: the neck may, in fact, be well positioned relative to the body; however, the imaginary line along the middle of the neck extends outward rather than upward. Some French-bred horses, in particular, and also some Thoroughbreds tend to have either horizontal or ewe-necks. In both cases, elevating the forehand, the quality of the horse's "mouth," and the general "rideability" of the horse becomes an issue.

Neck Muscling

As I pointed out earlier in this chapter, the KWPN (NA/WPN) lists "Muscling of Neck" as a separate conformational characteristic on the studbook's Linear Score Sheet. The desired neck consists of a rounded topline, and the under-part, from the throatlatch to the point of the shoulder, should display a nice, distinct "cut out" shape. This shape is not determined by bones but by soft tissue—muscles, in particular.

KWPN (NA/WPN) selection inspectors prefer not to see heavy muscling on the underside of the neck or a neck that is not nicely distinct where it joins the chest at its base. A slightly arched topline and sufficient length from the withers to the head make the art of riding easier for both horse and rider. It is remarkable what Anky van Grunsven says about Bonfire: "His neck is not ideal at all: it's skinny and poorly muscled." This is true: Bonfire's

neck is not ideal. However, it is certainly functional. It has length, natural upward curve of the imaginary line, and a refined head-neck connection. When trying to find dressage prospects, you learn not to complain if you find a horse with a neck like Bonfire's because something good can be made of it. Bonfire could collect and extend with his forehand; he could "climb" in the passage and bend in the shoulder-in; and he could deal with the positive tension created by the triangle of his rider's leg, seat, and hands exceptionally well.

This is an example of a horse with a "light," clean, or refined head-neck connection.

ANKY VAN GRUNSVEN

Riding Horses "Round"

I really don't disagree with anything in this chapter. I do, however, have several comments.

The poll must certainly be the highest point, but there are examples of very successful horses whose highest points were a bit behind the poll. If you really look at the famous dressage stallion Donnerhall, ridden by Karin Rehbein, that particular FEI rule didn't apply to him. Perhaps it had something to do with his "stallion" neck. We shouldn't make too much of a fuss over this in such cases; otherwise, we'll have to stop competing stallions.

In general, a heavy neck makes work with a horse more difficult. A big, arched neck certainly looks nice, but getting this type of horse to work "over his back" isn't so easy. The lack of flexibility in the neck affects the whole horse. A less heavy neck just makes things easier. The ideal is a long and correctly placed neck—then it's the rider's job to ride well. I also agree that heavy jowls are undesirable as they make correct contact more difficult to achieve.

The underside of the neck may be a matter of conformation, but it is usually created as a result of incorrect riding. Our training system is based on riding a horse "round," which if done properly, facilitates the correct neck muscle development. This does not mean that I only train horses by riding them low and round; variety is very important.

This horse has a clear, upward curve to his neck.

A Strong and Supple Topline

6

With respect to dressage horse conformation, "length" is almost the equivalent of functionality. The rules that apply to the legs and the neck also apply to the body. A dressage horse must show lateral flexion, bending easily around the rider's leg while trotting forward undisturbed in the same rhythm.

On this topic, the *FEI Rulebook* states the following: [*The horse remains*] *"absolutely straight in any movement on a straight line and bending accordingly when moving on curved lines."* This elasticity must originate somewhere: not from the horse's width but from his length. If you take two pieces of wood that are the same in type, thickness, and width, but that are different in length, and then compare the flexibility of the two pieces, you will see how this is in fact true.

Body Length

The KWPN (NA/WPN) considers the horse's length so important the question of "Body Shape" is very first on the Linear Score Sheet. This characteristic is evaluated by determining whether a horse is "square" or "rectangular." The horse's score is based on his total length relative to his height. A horse whose length is greater than his height is a rectangular type; a horse whose length equals his height is a square type. We strive for a long horse, which in general means a rectangular-type horse. To complicate matters, however, if a horse has long legs—a positive characteristic for a dressage horse, as we've discussed—he may be more of a square type.

The length of a horse should not only be measured by his back, but by the *whole* horse—after all, it is not just the barrel that bends around the rider's leg. In any case, the quest for length does have its limits. The longer the horse, the greater his mass; and the heavier the horse, the slower he moves. And, the length of the back affects its function as the "bridge" between the hindquarters and the forehand. Movement must start in the hindquarters and flow "over the back" to the front of the horse.

In addition, the horse must be able to manoeuvre his hind legs, and lift and lighten his forehand. This requires strength. The bridge between the hindquarters and the forehand is created by the topline (which will be discussed further), but the muscle group that runs along the bottom of the barrel, from croup to sternum, is just as important and deserves separate attention (see chapter 9, p. 43, for more information). For the time being, we can simply conclude that developing the desired "positive tension" in a long back requires more strength than a short back. Therefore, quality standards also *limit* the length of the horse's back. The desire to breed long, well-developed horses *should not* degenerate into breeding oddities.

The Function of the Back and Loins

Most of us know that a horse's power originates in the muscles of his hindquarters; however, few people realize that the shape and muscling of the back is very important to effectively transfer that power. This process can be compared to a car engine: a high-powered engine is of little use if it is not fitted with the right gearbox and clutch. The hindquarters generate

This horse is a square type.

Tineke Bartels' first Grand Prix horse Olympic Duco was a nice rectangular type, and his topline was distinguished by solid muscling.

power; the back transfers the power, and together, they produce the total athletic effort that is the foundation of dressage.

The horse's back does two things simultaneously: it contributes to the horse moving with an elevated forehand, which in theory becomes more difficult the greater the distance between the hindquarters and the forehand. At the same time, the back is vitally important for suppleness, a quality that is facilitated primarily by length. The back must be at once strong and supple, and solid and permeable. The horse's topline is a carrying construction of muscle and bone, each essential in making the other strong and supple.

Curvature

The double function of strength and suppleness requires not only that the length of the whole horse be well-proportioned but also that the horse's topline show a well-proportioned "curvature" from the withers

ANKY VAN GRUNSVEN

Contract and Relax

I do think long horses are attractive, but is body length *really* functional? Not if we're talking about a "backyard" horse. And, how long do we really want our horses? Can it be expressed in inches? Now, take Gestion Krack C, for example. He doesn't have a long back, and his legs are very long, so he is not the desired "rectangular-type," but he's certainly extremely elastic and definitely an athlete!

I can't say if long horses are more difficult to collect than short-backed ones. The horses I've had until now that have had problems with collection didn't have those problems because of conformation flaws but because of their slow way of moving. In my experience, training makes a back functional and well muscled. A horse will develop a better-muscled topline if he's consistently required to contract and relax those muscles. Of course, the horse must go in the classical frame at shows, working "over the back," but to bring a horse to the point where he is capable of this frame, you have to pay special attention to developing all of his muscles.

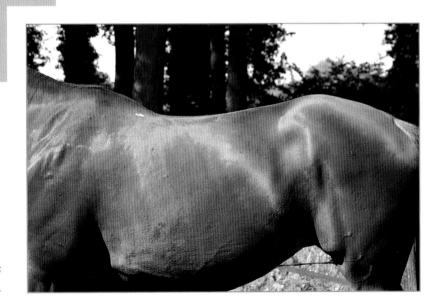

The muscles of this horse's topline need improvement.

A hollow back weakens the connection between the hindquarters and the forehand. This is a disadvantage because the strides generated by the hindquarters must be transferred to the forehand with rhythm and regularity.

to the tail. From the withers to the back, the topline should curve *downward* an equal amount to the curve *upward* from the back to the loins and croup. This upward curvature should not be too hollow, too round, or too rigid. As previously stated, muscles and bones make each other strong, but also supple. A rigid, fixed topline does not facilitate flexibility in movement, and legs that swing back and forth create motion that should be received and passed on in a supple manner.

Curvature is necessary for the energy generated by the horse's movement to flow through his body; however, *too much* curvature, in the form of a hollow back, weakens the connection between the hindquarters and the forehand—a disadvantage because the strides generated in the hindquarters must be transferred to the forehand with rhythm and regularity. Consider what often happens when a young dressage horse has to perform a simple lateral movement—the power flowing forward through the body from the motor in the rear comes to an abrupt halt halfway. The smallest disruption in power can lead to a rhythm mistake, so just imagine what happens when the flow of movement completely stops halfway!

The importance of a supple and strong connection between the hindquarters and the forehand is confirmed by the Linear Score Sheet, which judges both the "Line of the Back" and the "Line of the Loins."

A Croup to "Sit" On

Two major parts of the horse come together in the croup: the spinal column and the hind limbs. They represent the integration of propulsive and conveying forces.

A horse's croup is part of, and fully integrated into his topline, the physical "bridge" that conveys the carrying power developed by the hindquarters stepping under the horse's body to the forehand. As with the horse's back, the croup's length and muscling are integral to the system.

We will address the horse's hindquarters in two ways. In this chapter, we will first view the croup from a *horizontal* perspective, in conjunction with the horse's topline in its entirety. In the following chapter, we will take a *vertical* perspective as we discuss croup in relation to the hind legs.

Croup Length

Just as with other parts of the horse, we cannot measure the croup in inches but only in connection with and relative to the rest of the horse. We have already determined that the ideal ratio between the forehand, barrel, and hindquarters is 1: 1: 1. Unfortunately, figuring the length of the hindquarters is difficult. At what points on the horse do you start and end? The placement of the tail sometimes makes a visual assessment difficult. For example, if the tail is set high, then the croup appears short. To correctly assess croup length, we need to look from the point of the hip—the area that horses sometimes bump when they go through a stall doorway—to the point of the buttock (see the

illustration of the equine skeleton in chapter 5, p. 28).

The length of the croup is relative to its position: the more sloped the croup, the shorter the croup. However, the angle of the croup is not only significant to its length. As part of the topline, the angle of the croup determines the degree to which hind leg impulsion coordinates with the loins and back—and thus the rest of the horse by way of this bridge.

A Sloped Croup

For centuries, some breeds have been selected for their steeply sloped croups for a practical purpose: a tilted pelvis clearly helps a draft horse convert his huge muscle power into optimum pulling power. However, scientific research has shown that a steeply sloped croup hinders the movement of dressage horses. In 1994, Mikael Holmström asserted that good-moving dressage horses display greater pelvic activity than poor-moving horses. Holmström's study found pelvic flexibility to be the determining factor for the ability to passage. Steeply sloped hindquarters reduce the capacity for pelvic movement and a horse with a sloped croup has much more difficulty "sitting" in collected movements because he is already in the "sitting" position.

The *FEI Rulebook* states the following about the piaffe, in which the horse "sits" while trotting in place: *"The quarters are slightly lowered, the haunches with active hocks are well engaged, giving great freedom, lightness and mobility to the shoulders and forehand."*

In contrast, a completely flat croup is also undesirable, particularly for reasons of suppleness. The entire topline is responsible for coordinating the flow of movement that originates in the hind legs and ends in

The Freundentanzer son Farbenfroh's croup was rather flat, but that did not prevent him from winning the dressage world championship with Nadine Capellmann in Jerez, Spain, in 2002.

the use of the front legs. This coordination can be compared to that of an archer's bow. The curved shape and construct of a bow successfully combines flexibility and strength. Similarly, the horse's topline along the hindquarters requires a slight sloping line.

Of course, there are world champion horses with flat croups—but although Isabell Werth's Gigolo and Nadine Capellmann's Farbenfroh ranked among the world's best horses, flexibility (through their bodies) was definitely not their strongest point.

The Modern Riding Horse

For a long time, a sloped croup proved that a horse was bred for riding purposes. In the 1960s and 1970s, for example, the Gelderlander and Groninger horses had to be transformed into modern riding horses, and breeders at that time thought that a horse needed a sloped croup to use his hind legs well—they felt a sloped croup automatically placed the hind legs under the body. In fact, the ideal, and most functional, hind leg stance depends on the length and build of the entire hindquarters, not just the position of the pelvis.

ANKY VAN GRUNSVEN

"Pushing" Power versus "Carrying" Power

I think it is indeed logical that draft horses and Thoroughbreds have sloping croups because they've always have had to do work requiring *pushing off* power, while dressage horses mainly need *carrying* power. (Dressage does require a horse to both carry *and* push, but carrying is the more important of the two.) And honestly, I just don't care for the look of a sloping croup.

I really dislike what I call "waddling" hips. If you look at the top of a moving horse's croup, you should, of course, see it "swing," but the extent of that movement should be limited. If a croup doesn't stay relatively still while a horse moves, then I don't think it's very functional.

Finally, I completely agree that Gigolo and Farbenfroh, while fabulous dressage horses, were not very flexible due to their flat croups. Farbenfroh, for one, showed more flexibility in his legs than in his topline.

A tilted pelvis optimizes a draft horse's ability to convert his huge hind muscle power into pushing off power.

8 Hind Legs Built to Carry

To enable horses and riders to perform well, breeders try to produce horses with hind legs that naturally stand "under" the horse's body. Just as the front legs should naturally be situated at the front of the horse's body (rather than "under" it) to guarantee optimum stride completion, so should the hind legs easily move under the horse's body to best facilitate carrying power.

When looking at a horse standing "square" (evenly balanced on four legs), you could easily say, "The front legs and hind legs are *both* under the horse's body." The degree to which the front legs stand under the body should not be too great, as mentioned earlier, as such a fault in the front is often accompanied by a hind-legged stance that trails behind the body (although Gestion Bonfire, the 2000 Olympic champion, always stands with his hind legs feet behind his body). It really is best if this entire discussion regarding the base (the legs) under the mass (the body) is considered in connection with the horse in motion: each stride a horse takes begins with a forward movement of a leg; therefore, the *front* legs must move in *front* of the body and the *hind* legs *underneath* it.

The actual construction of the hind legs is best seen via radiographs (X rays). Bones that are readily visible in the human leg (such as the pelvis, hip joints, and femur) are not visible in the horse's—even the stifle is difficult to observe. Our hind leg analysis deals with two things: length and angles. These two elements determine the solidity and functionality of the hind end. (Moreover, they have a mutual relationship, for the angles of a triangle change as one side gets longer or shorter.) Although length and angles are closely related, I will first discuss these matters separately, and later draw conclusions regarding the whole subject.

Stifle Angle

The desired stance with the hind legs positioned slightly under the horse's body directly depends on the placement of the femur, which connects the hip joint to the stifle joint. A straight femur places the hind legs behind the body; a sloping femur places them under his body and enables the horse to lift and move his hind legs easily. Numerous scientific studies have demonstrated the importance of an angled femur, and Holmström (see earlier discussions, p. 24 and p. 35) found that horses with significantly straight femurs tend to have back and lameness problems.

The angle formed by the femur along with the tibia and fibula (with the point of this "triangle" being the stifle), should be slightly greater than 90 degrees. If this angle is too small, then the support function of the stifle joint is compromised and the tendons and ligaments around the joint are overly stressed by the concussion from each step of the hind legs.

The stifle's diminished ability to function as a support, and the related increased stress on the structures surrounding the joint leads to a reluctance to "close" the angles in the upper part of the hind legs. This type of stiffness is readily visible (lateral movement of the stifle can be observed easily in horses with this problem). Horses are mechanically made to "swing" their legs forward and backward. If this natural movement pattern is disturbed and a "sideways" movement is included within the joint, then the areas in and around the joints are subject to extra stress.

Hock Angle

There are three angles in the hind leg, but the one most often discussed is the angle created by the hock because it is readily visible. Although the three angles of the hind leg are closely related to one another, and the hock is how we determine whether a horse is "sickle-hocked" or straight behind, it is narrow-minded to use it exclusively when assessing a horse's hind legs.

The same rules apply to the angle of the hock that apply to the angle of the stifle: a small angle (sickle-hocked) reduces this joint's ability to support the horse and increases the stress on the structures surrounding the joint. Scientific research has shown higher percentages of lameness and back problems occur in horses that are sickle-hocked.

In Holmström's research in 1990 on a group of dressage horses, he found none of them had a narrow hock angle; however, wider angles—and subsequently straighter hind legs—did not necessarily produce better hind legs. Decidedly straight hind legs are actually associated with several significant problems. First, a direct correlation exists between larger hock angles and high hindquarters: it can sometimes be observed that horses built on the forehand are that way partially as a result of having straight hind legs.

The second problem with straight hind legs is they often result in weak pasterns. The uneven distribution of downward forces (discussed on p. 24) takes its toll on the pastern joints, which adversely affects a horse's long-term use.

Moreover, there is often a correlation between straight hind legs and limited bend of the hocks—a very negative quality for dressage horses that need to be able to use their hind legs expressively in order to earn high scores.

When assessing a horse's hocks, it is perhaps best to remember the old Dutch saying, "The middle road is paved in gold." Both sickle-hocked and extremely

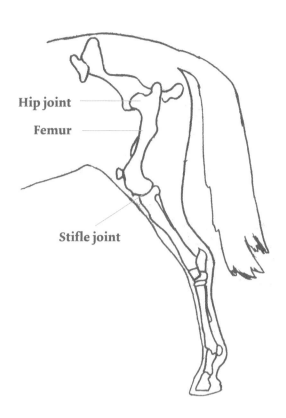

The femur in this illustration is very straight, resulting in hind legs that trail behind the body (camped-out). The slope of the femur is difficult to determine with the human eye; however, a good approximation can be made by drawing an imaginary line from the hip joint (just in front of the point of the buttock) to the stifle joint.

straight hind legs are undesirable. In practice, breeders strive for a hock angle of about 150 degrees.

Hind Leg Length

Up to this point, I've based the discussion of the hind leg on the premise of a correctly proportioned horse—a horse with hind legs of a normal length. However, the influence of the Thoroughbred, in particular, introduced long hind legs into western European sport horse breeding. Selective breeding for speed over the last three centuries promoted long hind legs in the Thoroughbred breed. This gave them the power to increase their stride length at their maximum stride frequency, enabling them to win races. Long hind legs

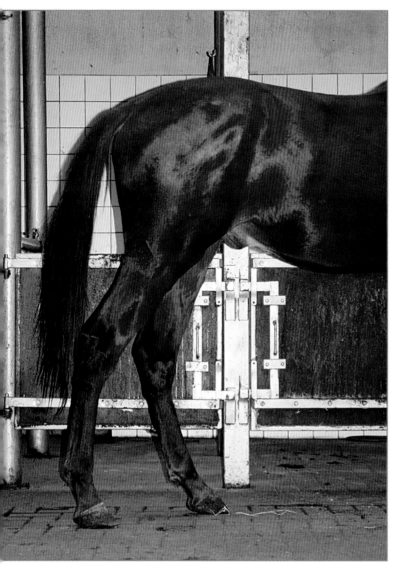

Scientific research has shown that horses with sickle-hocked hind legs have a tendency for back and lameness problems.

have, therefore, become a distinctive trait of the Thoroughbred and now something we also deal with when breeding Warmbloods.

Disproportionately long hind legs often cause the horse to be built on the forehand, and they tend not to stand under the body as they should. The excess length often leads to poor hind leg angles and subsequently stresses weak parts around the joints. From a purely mechanical perspective, it is more difficult for a moving horse to bring long hind legs under his body far enough or quickly enough to score well in competitive

dressage, although some horses do indeed have the "heart" necessary to deal with this physical limitation and use their long hind legs as powerful weapons for extra reach and driving power.

It is important to look at the relationships between the different parts of the horse's hind end. There are horses with long cannons and short cannons, and horses with long gaskins and short gaskins. Relatively low set hocks are associated with longer gaskins and shorter cannons—proportions that, from a mechanical perspective, are conducive to developing strong, powerful hindquarters. For example, horses with low set hocks can "sit" easier in the piaffe.

Spring Action

The lowest joints of the horse's hind legs tend to be neglected in discussion. This is odd because the horse owes a great deal of its unique ability to what Stephan Budiansky calls the "springing foot" in his book *The Nature of Horses* (Free Press, 1997). As the hooves of a moving horse contact the ground, the superficial flexor tendons function as elastic bands that stretch, absorbing the shock of landing and storing up a significant amount of energy for a short time. Then, in the following phase of movement, the "springing foot" recoils to release and use the stored energy.

When Wim Back, DVM (Faculty of Veterinary Medicine at Utrecht University in the Netherlands), conducted researched on biomechanics and used "markers" to take objective measurements of horse's movement, Ab Barneveld, DVM (Assistant Professor in Equine Surgery of the Faculty of Veterinary Medicine at Utrecht University in the Netherlands), was present as a subjective observer. Barneveld found that greater movement was consistent with rather weak, very elastic pasterns. This scientifically proven, positive correlation between pastern elasticity and dressage ability is in complete agreement with the practical findings of riders, trainers, and breeders of dressage horses.

A horse's pasterns flex and recoil countless times over the span of his life. Time and again, the considerable weight of the horse's body rests on these relatively small shock absorbers. Furthermore, in the trot, piaffe, and passage the dressage horse's entire weight rests on only two "springing feet." It is clear that we place extremely high demands on this part of the horse's body, both in the front and hind legs, and thus "Stance of Pasterns" rightly judges both length and elasticity on the KWPN (NA/WPN) Linear Score Sheet.

Two important points concerning pastern elasticity must be balanced:

1. The flexibility with which energy traveling downward (landing phase) is converted into energy moving upward (lift-off phase).

2. The strength of the foundation (the pasterns). Just as with the previously discussed lengths and angles, one most know "how much is too much" flexibility. A clearly weak pastern is very susceptible to injury, and the longer the pastern, the more flexible or weak (although there are also short and weak pasterns). Furthermore, scientific research has shown an

increased risk of injury to both long, weak pasterns and short, straight pasterns.

Breeders like to see a pastern ranging in length from sufficient to long with a slight slope (see chapter 4, p. 000). A horse's pasterns can be assessed by drawing an imaginary line from the bottom of the hoof through the pastern. This line should be unbroken.

When viewing a horse from behind, you will see that the hind feet are turned toes-outward a few degrees. A completely straight hind leg stance is unnatural. When the horse moves, the hind legs swing up and alongside the front legs, and the asymmetrical effect on the centrally located center of gravity, as discussed on p. 000, also plays a part.

A horse that stands with his hind toes turned too far outward is called "cow-hocked." The hocks are set too close to each other, and the horse moves with wide stifles, which is undesirable, as soft tissues are subjected to extra stress.

The angle in this horse's hock joint is greater than the ideal 150 degrees.

ANKY VAN GRUNSVEN

Elastic Pasterns

We got the shock of our lives just after we bought Bonfire: he dug a trench with his front feet that was so deep his belly touched the ground and his hind legs stood in a corner! We thought something was seriously wrong with him! He had already passed the vet check, but I had him completely vetted one more time because his behavior was definitely not normal. Bonfire was two-and-a-half years old at that time—but to this day, he'll dig a trench if given a chance!

In addition to his practice of digging holes, during award ceremonies Bonfire would stand very strangely with his hind legs stretched out about 3 feet behind him. Sjef would usually call out, "He's not allowed to do that!" But what could I do? Actually, Bonfire is not the only horse I've known with such a strange habit; Gere would often do the same thing.

I've often discussed Bonfire's elastic pasterns with my brother. They flex so much his pastern joints touch the ground. "That certainly can't be good for him," my brother insists, but Bonfire has aged in good health despite this. I must admit that I have never asked him to piaffe for extended periods, although he certainly could.

I understand the legitimacy of the reference to the Dutch saying about the "golden middle road," but practice is sometimes a bit different than theory. For example, Gestion Joker had very straight hind legs, but as I've said before, the way a horse moves matters more to me than the way he looks. I have to like his movement—and Joker bent and used his very straight hind legs extremely well.

On the other hand, I've had bad experiences with horses with extremely angled hind legs. They tend to be difficult to collect for a pirouette or piaffe. Their hind legs come too far under their bodies, which leads to problems with balance.

And, I'm really pleased that this chapter includes the illustration on p. 39; it clarifies the position of the femur for me! I don't know how anyone can see if a horse really has a straight or sloped femur—there must be a trick to it!

Built like an Archer's Bow and String 9

Up to now in this book about the conformation, movement, and temperament of the dressage horse, the horse's muscling has been relegated to a secondary position after the form of the skeleton. This should not actually be the case because a dressage horse is all about movement, and bones do not generate movement—only muscles do.

Since the horse's muscles are so important, this chapter deals with them specifically. However, the horse's drive power (movement) cannot be separated from:

1. The system that "automatically" holds the horse's body in balance.
2. The horse's ability to round his topline by lifting his back and/or hollow his back by dropping it.

For these two reasons, this chapter also deals with the principle that the entire horse is built like an archer's bow and string. From the perspective of the topline and the line that runs under the belly—which hold one another taut like a bow and string—the horse is a complex system comprised of mutually dependent muscles, ligaments, tendons, and bones.

In 1946, the Dutch zoologist E.J. Slijper put an end to the false conception that the primary function of the horse's back was as a "bridge." The original line of thinking only considered the spinal column and its immediate structures (the topline), and therefore was incomplete. Slijper thought that the entire body (in other words, the topline and the "underline") had to be included in the concept and discovered that the mutual tension of an archer's bow and string adequately represented the actual structures of the horse's body.

The Topline: The Bow

The horse's spinal column—in particular, the back, the loins and the structures surrounding these—work as the bow. One of the most important parts of this bow is a grouping of many small muscles, heavily interleaved (layered) with tiny tendons that run from the front of the horse to his tail. This muscle group is responsible for sensing the horse's bodily stance and making necessary corrections, a system that allows a horse—like a person—to keep his balance even with his eyes closed.

The topline (the bow) includes other muscles: those I call the "back-stretchers." These muscles in the back and loins fulfill one main task: to make the back hollow. The bow is stretched to its maximum tension when the horse raises his head and neck (and thus the front part of the spinal column) and does the same with his tail, completely tightening the back. As a result of this, the hind legs cannot optimally step under the horse's body, and coming full circle, the curtailed hind leg activity then makes it difficult for the horse to lift his back.

In addition to extending the back and loins, the muscles along the topline function to bend the spinal column in a turn or during lateral movement. This explains why horses with a hollow topline or poor back and loin muscling often have difficulty with rhythm and regularity in the lateral movements. A horse with a hollow back is naturally always at a disadvantage when it comes to achieving collection.

The Underline: The String

The string on an archer's bow keeps the bow in a fixed

position of constant tension, and the muscles of the "underline" (the underside of the neck, chest, stomach, and the insides of the hind limbs) serve a similar purpose in regards to the horse's spinal column (the "bow" in my metaphor). The primary function of this bow-and-string construction is to maintain balance. A horse has a central balance system that works automatically through the continuous measuring of muscle tension, a system that is disturbed when the rider sits on the horse's back. This explains why almost all horses display uncharacteristically poor movement when they are first started under saddle. The horse's movement generally improves once progressive training restores his balance.

Variable Tension

Before looking at exactly which muscle groups are responsible for the dressage horse's most important movements, there are a few observations to make in response to the bow-and-string construction. In addition to the more or less constant tension between the topline and the underline, there is also variable tension created by the horse's movement, or to be precise, through the activity of the *protractors* (the muscles that pull the legs forward) and the *retractors* (the muscles that pull the legs backward). When a horse moves, the swinging motion of his legs creates a *dynamic* system, with varying amounts of tension and several popular ways to describe it (for example, working "through the body" or "over the back"). When the *hind legs* move *forward* and *front legs* move *backward*, the "bow" tenses and the back rounds. When the front legs move forward and hind legs move backward, the "string" tenses and the back stretches, or hollows.

First and foremost, it is important for dressage horse trainers to establish that activating the hind legs and bringing them under the body via the bow-and-string principle positively affects the topline by making it round and loose. Lowering the head promotes a round topline, as well, while raising the horse's head makes the topline hollow. Furthermore, a round and loose topline actually enables the hind legs to maximally step under the horse—and so a circle is completed.

A Neck that Arches Upward

Biomechanics confirms what many riders feel: a neck that arches sufficiently upward from the shoulder has a positive effect on a horse's ability to move "through his body" in a relaxed way. It is easier for a horse with such a neck to go "long and low" than it is for a horse with a horizontal neck to move in a collected frame, as the horse will tend to tighten his topline. Unlike the underline, the muscles of the topline remain largely disconnected while the horse is in motion and are not responsible for making the back round and loose.

"Over the Back"

Moving "over the back" in a relaxed way is an important goal of dressage, as stated in **Article 401, paragraph 1–2.2** of the *FEI Rulebook*: "*...it makes the horse supple, loose and flexible, but also confident, attentive and keen, thus achieving perfect understanding with his rider. These qualities are revealed by the freedom and regularity of the paces; the harmony, lightness and ease of the movements.*"

It's no wonder that good trainers give so much attention to "moving over the back." The rider uses connection to ask for collection, and thus tests the level of the horse's training and the quality of movement—but connection necessitates activating the hind legs, and with that, bending, rounding, and loosening the topline. In order for a horse to perform the exercises and achieve the required degree of collection, the horse's body—sometimes only accomplished after years of training—must ultimately show it can move with an elevated forehand. However, all too often we see the rider's hands forcing an elevated forehand, which results in an irrevocably tight and dropped back. The long ascent to Grand Prix should be represented by the horse's body slowly learning how to elevate, based on "carrying" hind legs, which keep the topline loose.

We are now completely in the realm of trainers and this book is meant to focus primarily on aspects of the dressage horse pertinent to breeding science—that is, inherited abilities. Unfortunately, we will develop moving round and "over the back" as a heritable trait. However, it was necessary to deal with the bow-and-string principle, related muscle groups, and their influence on the forward-moving horse.

Invisible Propellants

We only see a small portion of where movement originates in the horse's body. We can see very few of the many muscles that are vital to high quality movement. Breeders are thus inclined to ascribe all quality to the visible muscles of the back, loins, croup, and hindquarters. We need to learn to distill the effectiveness of a horse's muscling from two areas: the muscles we can actually see and the way the horse moves. (We can use the latter to determine the quality of those muscles we cannot see.) In fact, a moving horse gives the viewer sufficient information.

We can observe the muscles of the hindquarters, which are largely responsible for the horse's drive power, hind leg "push," and "buoyancy" of stride. Experience has taught breeders that good sport horses always have long, well-developed hindquarter muscles, which makes complete sense if you look at that muscle group's job and the great significance of that

job: every sport horse needs power and impulsion.

However, what the hindquarter muscles do that we cannot see is just as important. The quadriceps muscle group is largely hidden behind the stifle, and we can only estimate its quality by seeing a horse move. It brings the hind legs forward, and so is essential to bringing the hindquarters under the horse's body.

The Rear Engine

We know that the horse's "motor" is in the rear (the hindquarters), and this is where his movement begins. However, we don't buy a car because it has a nice engine; we buy it because we like how it drives.

The movement starts from the rear and goes forward, and is a cooperative effort of all the body's parts. The hindquarter muscles and back muscles are linked together, and as a result, the movement from the motor is transmitted forward and the front legs are activated. Muscles that extend from the throatlatch through the underside of the neck to the front legs are responsible for moving the front legs forward (protraction), while the triceps muscle, which is hidden behind the shoulder blade, functions as the retractor. Muscles in the gaskin stretch and bend the lower hind leg.

Protraction (top) and retraction (bottom) of the hind legs.

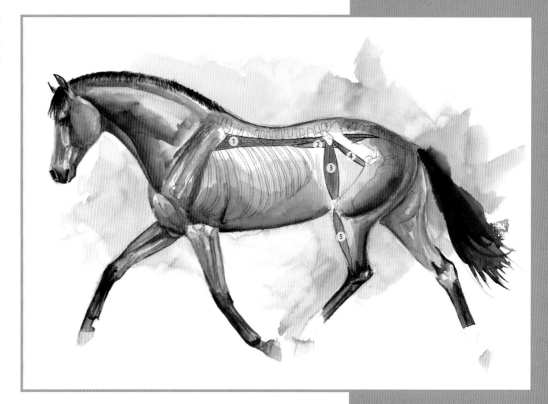

1   M. longissimus lumborum
2   M. psoas
3   M. tensor fasciae latae
4   M. gluteus profundus
5   M. extensor digitalis
    longus
6   M. rectus abdominis
7   M. gluteus superficialis
8   M. biceps femoris
9   M. semitendinosis
10 M. biceps femoris caudalis
11 M. semimembranosis
12 M. brachiocephalicus
13 M. pectoralis profundus
14 M. subscapularis
15 M. extensor carpi radialis
16 M. subscapularis
17 M. deltoideus
18 M. biceps brachii
19 M. subclavius
20 M. triceps brachii
21 M. extensor carpi ulnaris

*Protraction (top)
and retraction
(bottom) of the
front legs.*

ANKY VAN GRUNSVEN

Low and Round

Anyone who has heard Sjef and I talk about riding and training dressage horses will understand why I think this is a great chapter. Those who understand the art of dressage are best prepared to read this chapter and draw only one conclusion: that this is how a horse works, so this is how you can best ride him. It's a matter of contracting and relaxing, discovering how far you can go in a specific phase of training and then backing off and giving the horse time to absorb it all.

Despite this, the public debate about riding low and round—with the main contention being that this should be considered a form of animal abuse—continues! I have excellent proof at my barn that riding low and round only contributes to a horse's well-being: he's well over twenty years old, totally healthy, and his name is Bonfire.

What bothers me most about this debate is that some people criticize riding low and round by referencing only the incorrect way of doing it (with the horse's nose pulled tightly against his chest). We will always find ways to criticize many things as it is in our human nature, but the obvious point here is that rid-

ing incorrectly, whether it is low and round or in a tightly collected frame, is always wrong. I've said this before, and I'll say it again: one should thoroughly understand the subject he or she is debating before criticizing others.

When it comes to making a horse's topline round, I notice differences from horse to horse. One horse's back is easier to loosen through training than another's. I also see great differences between training today and work done in years prior. It used to be that you were quite happy if you could ride the required movements, and getting the back loose simply wasn't a priority. Fortunately, this mentality has considerably improved, and horses now progress to Grand Prix working "over the back."

Different training methods exist, and I'm not one to contend that someone else's method is unsuccessful or cruel to animals. I will say that riding low and round "fits" with a horse's conformation, and this method has continuously produced the best results over the years. Rembrandt, Corlandus, and Isabell Werth's horses—and let's not forget Schockemöhle and Beerbaum's jumpers—are all trained low and round.

A schematic representation of the bow-and-string construction. Included are the factors that influence the tightening and loosening of the "bow."

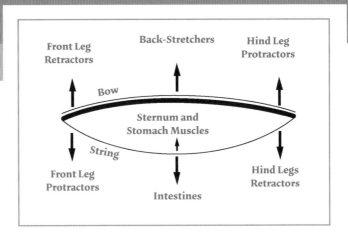

These illustrations depict two opposite moments of variable tension within the bow-and-string construction. (Top) The hind leg is placed far under the body and the low head position stretches the horse's topline, making it round and flexible.

Here, the horse is hollowing his back because he is coming against the rider's hand. He brings his head up high, and as a result, stretches the "underline." A hollow topline adversely affects the horse's ability to bring his hind legs underneath his body.

movement

10 The Importance of Movement

There is not a single horse in existence that does not move—apart from Amor, Julio Mariner, Deister, and a handful of other horses that were so unique in life, statues have been made in their likeness. In fact, only the horses that distinguish themselves as world-class movers are ever cast in bronze, destined to stand in one place for centuries in recognition of their unparalleled movement.

Evolution transformed the first horse, a slow, rummaging forest dweller, into a lightning quick range animal. The four feet that originally left pad-and-toe imprints in the moist earth changed over thousands of millennia, eventually becoming long, slender legs, with only "nails" (hooves) leaving scratches on the dried-up ground. Initially, Mother Nature equipped the horse with only one weapon for survival: the ability to move across long distances in little time. But nowadays, what once was a weapon actually threatens the horse's well-being should he fall into the hands of an individual who does not recognize his movement as imperative. A horse *must* move; otherwise, he suffers adverse physical consequences. It's reassuring to think that riding dressage combines enjoyment with purpose!

Up to this point, we have mainly dealt with the dressage horse's conformation. We *did not* specifically deal with the conformation of a still horse, standing square—although this may have seemed to be the case, the reference to the horse in movement was made repeatedly. We do not strive for a long-necked, uphill-built dressage horse because these characteristics meet a traditional ideal of physical beauty, but because a horse with these particular conformational traits can perform better. Whether or not they actually *do* perform better depends on the quality of their basic gaits, among other things.

Completing Conformational Evaluation

We cannot predict the value of a dressage horse that is standing still, but we certainly can if he is moving! We can use movement to complete our evaluation of the horse's conformation. What's really happening with his neck? Does he really use it correctly? Does the horse with the tight topline really lack flexibility? We cannot make any pronouncement about a horse until we have seen him move. For this very reason, we must consider the whole horse and not just his individual characteristics. For example, consider Robin Hood, winner of the 2003 PAVO Cup Finals for five-year-old dressage horses in Ermelo, the Netherlands. This son of Jazz was relatively small and undeveloped when initially compared to his big, flashy competition in the final; however, when the 16.1-hand Robin Hood started moving, he seemed to grow another four inches! Based on the way he moved, he was both the most talented and the most beautiful in his class.

How often do we say, "But you should see how nice he is when he moves!"? These words are related to the late KWPN Head Inspector Gert van der Veen's favorite saying when he talked about a horse's movement: "Beauty is as beauty does." Breeders do not like a long, arched neck because it inspired Michelangelo to create fine art but because a long neck serves dressage riders well.

52

Sound Assessment

We know if a horse has "good" potential when he begins to move, and we can make some rather sound assessments based on simply seeing him loose in an arena. This does not mean we can predict the career of each individual horse at age three; however, we can make rather good distinctions between the better and poorer quality three-year-olds by evaluating large numbers of horses. This appeared to be the case when we connected KWPN studbook inspection movement scores for three-year-olds to the same horses' future dressage performance.

A "correlation" is a way to measure how associated or related two variables are. In a *positive* correlation, as the value of one variable increases or decreases, the values of the other increases or decreases. So, a horse with high studbook inspection scores that eventually earns top dressage scores, or a horse that receives low scores at a keuring that struggles in the arena later would be examples of a *positive correlation.*

On the tables that appear on the following pages, a "0" would represent no relation between traits, and a "1" would be a perfect positive correlation.

Table 1 » Genetic correlation between the Studbook Score for "Movement" in Three-Year-Olds and Dressage Performance

Competitive Dressage	
SCORED MOVEMENT	*0.69

Based on the relatively high correlation between the score for "movement" and future competitive dressage performance, we may conclude that the qualities we see in three-year-old horses, moving at liberty, are largely the same as those that determine if a horse can succeed later in competition.

In past years, the major European sport horse breeders have conducted a great deal of research on the genetic connection between scored movement and dressage tal-

If Amor and his offspring had not been spectacular movers, a statue would never have been erected in his honor.

ent. If we place the data from all that research in a row, it appears that there is a correlation of 0.7 between the general judged trait "movement" and dressage ability (see Table 1). We also find a significant genetic connection between early movement and later performance in dressage. These are "reasonably sound assessments" we make of young horses—nothing more and nothing less. A moving horse can reveal to us—much more than his static body can—if he will be able to perform later dres-

53

When the 16.1-hand PAVO Cup winner Robin Hood started moving, he seemed to grow another four inches! Based on his movement, he was both the best and the most beautiful three-year-old in his class.

sage exercises with ease or if he will struggle. (If horses are able to perform dressage movements with ease, we will stress their minds less.) All of this information means we can use careful selection to breed horses with a specific talent for movement.

The Purpose of Selection

By analyzing movement, we can draw exactly the same conclusions about young horses embarking on a career

in dressage and breeding as we drew earlier by studying their conformation. Measured over generations and based on very general functional qualities, we are now able to breed a dressage horse that is better able to do his work. Selection based on acceptance into the studbook has already significantly contributed to improving dressage horse breeding.

However, we need to do more. Performance tests and higher levels of dressage make it naturally easier for breeders to locate the mares and stallions with the greatest dressage talent. (The inspection scores for each basic gait do show a somewhat less significant connection to later performances in competitive dressage than the total value of the "movement" category—see p. 53.) This makes sense because dressage performance depends on many factors, not just the quality of one basic gait.

Table 2 » **Genetic Correlation between Trait Scores from Performance Tests and Dressage Show Scores in the Netherlands and throughout Europe***

| | Competition | |
MPT	The Netherlands	Europe
WALK	0.27	0.4
TROT	0.62	0.7
CANTER	0.34	0.5
RIDING TEST	0.47	0.8

*In 1995, Arjen van Veldhuizen found satisfactory correlations between early evaluation of the trot and later success in competitive dressage, as well as a connection between scores in inspection riding tests and competitive dressage. The overall European figures are in line with the Dutch figures stated here—and some are even better. (This may be due to the larger quantity of data.) There is a high correlation between scores in the riding test and success in competitive dressage because the riding test looks specifically at the elements that are fundamentally crucial to the sport.

The correlations in Table 2 are based on the results of the Mare Performance Test (MPT). In fact, a somewhat older study (Huizinga) showed a similarly high correlation (0.83) between the competitive performances of stallions' offspring and the corresponding traits of those stallions as scored in the performance test.

In addition to the distinct relationship between a horse's early movement and his later performance in competition, the rate of quality in the three basic gaits also demonstrates a degree of connection. In terms of heredity, this means that the desired movement traits of dressage horses can be systematically selected.

Table 3 A » Genetic Correlation between Basic Gaits in the MPT (the Netherlands)*

	Walk	Trot	Canter
WALK			
TROT	0.79		
CANTER	0.55	0.78	

Table 3 B » Genetic Correlation between Basic Gaits in the MPT (Europe)*

	Walk	Trot	Canter
WALK			
TROT	0.6-0.7		
CANTER	0.6-0.7	0.7-0.8	

*Here are correlation scores representing the relationship between traits (in this case, the basic gaits). High scores between the basic gaits have been measured in the Netherlands and other countries, suggesting that successfully selecting one basic gait provides a genetic "entryway" for the other basic gaits.

It is not so peculiar that the horse's three gaits demonstrate a mutual relationship; aside from uncharacteristic, solitary examples and possibly poor rider influence, why would a horse show a great deal of flexibility in the walk and yet be stiff in his other gaits? Why would he be quick with his hind legs in the trot, but slow in his other gaits?

There are, of course, quality differences between an individual horse's basic gaits—a horse certainly does not receive the same score for each gait on his performance test. Some stallions do pass on one particular gait to their offspring very consistently; for example, Jazz's trot and Ferro's canter. On average, the other gaits these stallions pass on are also very solid, but then a "7" looks poor when compared to a "9" or "10"!

Usually, only the best stallions cover a lot of mares, thus providing us with a large number of offspring and therefore a great deal of information about their ability to pass on specific traits. We see very positive traits in their offspring as well as less desirable ones—and because there are more offspring, this might actually lead to criticism of that stallion, although only because of his success as a stud.

The genetic correlations between movement and conformation traits hover around "0" and thus are insignificant in terms of systematic breeding, and we won't even talk about the *negative* correlations between "jumping" and "dressage."

Conclusions

We may summarize the complex discussion of genetic predisposition in this chapter by drawing two simple conclusions:

1. It is a good idea to select young dressage horses by evaluating their movement.
2. Characteristics used when selecting dressage prospects are subsequently strengthened from generation to generation.

ANKY VAN GRUNSVEN

There's *Something* about That Horse!

It is often said that the best dressage horse is the most beautiful one. I would restate that as, "The best dressage horse is the one that makes the biggest impression." As far as I'm concerned, that's what our sport is about. It's not about a nice trot or a good canter: a really good dressage horse has to catch your eye, has to make you say, "Wow, there's something about that horse!" He may, in fact, be a very ordinary looking horse in his stall, just as there are very pretty horses that are entirely unremarkable in the dressage arena.

I can appreciate predictive values concerning movement as illustrated in this chapter. I've found that very often after many years of careful training, you're ultimately again faced with the same qualities you noticed in the horse at a very young age. I'm not only talking about negative qualities—a horse that shows a great canter or an exceptional extended trot at liberty won't lose those qualities under saddle with a good trainer. And, while you can improve a horse's specific weak areas through training, in the end, that improvement won't be enough to be truly competitive.

Just what is "good" movement, exactly? People have different tastes. Not everyone looks for the same type of movement in a horse. I discuss this in depth later in the book, but I'll briefly tell you what I look for: first and foremost, I look for a horse with quick and strong hind legs. All my horses have nice front leg action, but a dressage horse works from his hind end. Grand Prix level dressage is an extra tough job for a horse without a good motor.

I haven't really seen or experienced the genetic connection professed to exist between the basic gaits in this chapter. Naturally, these stated connections are based on data from many horses, and I suppose in theory, I have lately dealt with better horses in general in both my riding and teaching. But in my particular situation, differences in quality between a horse's basic gaits have more significance than they do in the general population.

I'm honestly a bit concerned about the fact that it's still difficult to find horses with three good, solid basic gaits. I'm not talking top-notch but simply gaits a trainer can work with. I'm afraid breeders still have work to do.

Natural Qualities

In the previous chapter, we saw that—where genetics are concerned—similarities between the three basic gaits are much more important than differences. For this reason, we will now discuss the horse's movement in general, and later, we will deal with the specific characteristics of each gait.

Conventional wisdom stating that the walk and the canter have more in common than the walk and trot, or trot and canter, was discounted in the previous chapter by recorded research. But, where did that idea originate? Is it an "old wives' tale" that's entirely untrue? The correlation figures listed in the previous chapter representing the degree of genetic relationship between the three basic gaits do not lie; however, there are solid similarities between the walk and the canter that distinguish them from the trot. The horse naturally uses his back much more in the walk and canter than in the trot. I will return to this point later in the book.

Breeding for Gaits

During the period when careful breeding transformed the horse to that which we are familiar with as the modern riding horse, breeders identified this similarity between the walk and the canter. They used the English Thoroughbred because the breed's walk and canter showed flexibility and rideability. On average, the Thoroughbred is a horse that can walk and canter well, while tending to have a mediocre trot. On the other hand, the Gelderlander horse, in particular, was selected and used for its strong show trot. For many generations now, breeders have successfully selected

for specific dressage qualities and if we continue to do our work well, breeding for the improvements desired, then we do not have to be concerned (given the correlation figures) that over time we will produce a "trotting machine" that can no longer walk and canter, or a "cantering wonder" born without a trot.

It has been said that the walk and the canter are the horse's two natural gaits, and the trot is a movement created by man. This is an interesting view if you consider that the old *FEI Rulebook* stated—almost at the beginning—that dressage helps improve the horse's natural qualities, and of all the horse's natural qualities, the basic gaits are certainly the most important.

If we look at a Standardbred trotter, a Hackney, or a carriage horse, it is difficult to call their way of moving "natural," which may be why the trot is considered a less natural gait. However, the Thoroughbred's canter strides are several feet longer than those of the original horse, and this has not transformed the canter, generally speaking, into an unnatural gait! Obviously, we do not have videos from the year 4000 B.C., but we see zebras and Przewalski horses walk, trot, and canter and can assume that these three gaits are part of these creatures' natural abilities. What riders and drivers do is cultivate. Training is used to develop a longer stride, as well as the ability to shorten strides, and this happens to all three gaits.

Three Reasons for Transitions

Under natural circumstances, the moment of transition from one basic gait to another is determined by speed, energy, and distribution of downward forces. The horse must move from the walk to the trot or canter if he wants to move faster than approximately three to four miles per hour. The horse can only go faster by developing a moment of suspension.

The difference in speed between the trot and the canter is relatively small: today, top trotters are almost as fast as top racehorses. Nevertheless, Mother Nature thought it necessary to let the horse choose between the canter and the trot, and zoological research has shown that horses transition from trot to canter to save energy (Hoyt and Taylor, 1981).

In the early nineties, when Claire T. Farley and C. Richard Taylor measured the downward forces involved in the horse's movement using a scale, they found that horses always transition from the trot to the canter at the point of maximum stress to their legs. Horses were tested with heavy weights, rested, and then tested again, and they transitioned from trot to canter at low speeds at the point of maximum stress, although from an energy conservation perspective, that transition was not desired. It is actually quite logical that a horse—upon increasing his speed and thus also increasing the downward forces impacting his legs—would rather distribute stress over three contact points with the ground (the canter) than over two (the trot).

Is It Natural?

Competitive dressage imposes very different limits on the horse's use of his gaits. Riders and trainers do not consider the ideal distribution of forces; they do not want to go from "A" to "B" using minimum energy. In contrast, they train the horse to trot with a huge explosion of energy at the very moment the horse would nat-

Improving the horse's "natural qualities" is an important discussion to engage in as riders, trainers, and breeders. We must consider our equine partner's abilities and needs when we use him for sport. On the left, the approved Icelandic stallion Bragi van Aldenghoor demonstrates the tölt. On the right, the KWPN-bred Gestion Goliath (Zebulon x Nieuwpoort), ridden by Arjen Teeuwissen, is performing the piaffe in the dressage stadium in Aachen, Germany.

ANKY VAN GRUNSVEN

Purpose

The walk and the canter have one very important thing in common: they can only be slightly improved by a rider. On the other hand, one can cultivate the trot, although the horse must have a sufficient trot to start because no matter how good you are, you can't turn a weak, expressionless pony-trot into one that is spectacular. If the horse has the basic trot, it can indeed be improved through training, much more than can the walk and the canter.

I really don't have much to say about the use of the word "natural" as debated in this chapter. Previously, we fought wars on horseback; now we do half-pass and tempi changes or jump a course of five-foot fences. I think *all* these things have little to do with nature. I feel it's far more important that work with horses has *purpose*. The horse served a pur-

pose for Native Americans—they used horses for hunting. Horses were once indispensable to farmers, who used them for various kinds of work from early in the morning to late at night. Today, the horse's purpose is related to sport and recreation or therapeutic work.

Some people, like myself, earn a living with horses, and that is just as valid a purpose as is the intense enjoyment pleasure riders get from their horses. I'm doubly fortunate because I not only earn my living with horses, I still enjoy riding as much as ever. I'd willingly give up everything else, but working with horses is what makes me happy. Without that happiness, I never could have sustained the pace of life I have these past years. And, I know for certain that this feeling of happiness is mutually dependent: I can't be happy riding a horse if that horse doesn't enjoy his work.

urally canter, and to collect his stride and trot almost in place when he is perhaps inclined to come to a halt. Or, the horse is trained to canter at the moment he would naturally come to a walk. In this sense, there is little that is "natural" about competitive dressage, which raises questions regarding the FEI principle that dressage "improves a horse's natural qualities." The FEI precept makes it sound as though it is immoral to do things with a horse that are unnatural, but horse sports are only immoral if we do not consider the needs and abilities of our equine partners—for instance, attempting to make a jumper out of a dressage horse or demanding a horse without any talent for dressage perform exercises that he hates.

Thriving with People

Perhaps the FEI intended to make the complex issue of equine natural ability "fit into" the lives of humans. Apparently, evolution has developed the horse in a way that makes him very suited to thriving in the proximity of people and cooperating with them. Without this natural ability to work for people, without people acting as the horse's keeper and "herd leader," perhaps the zebra would now be the sole representative of the horse family. It does not matter if a horse is used to tölt or piaffe, as long as a well-bred Icelandic horse is used for the tölt and a good dressage horse is used for the piaffe.

59

12 The Walk: Incorrect or Brilliant?

We have established the most important points concerning the horse in motion: he must move as Mother Nature intended him to; his "natural" (or in this case, *inherent*) way of moving must be suited to his job (i.e. dressage, carriage driving, endurance); and there are more similarities than differences between the three basic gaits. Now, let's take a close look at the foundation of the basic gaits.

Simply analyzing the gaits is not enough. The human eye is not suited to fully appreciate something as complicated as a moving horse. For centuries, false theories circulated about the footfall sequences and the degree to which different legs overlap during each phase of each gait. It seemed to be impossible to aptly describe the movement process—one that is measured in time and space—with only the naked eye as a tool. Now, thanks to an eccentric but brilliant pioneer of photography, we finally know the answers to questions as simple as "Does a moment exist during which all four of the horse's feet are off the ground?" In 1878, using a series of twenty-four photos taken with twenty-four different cameras and using strings to snap the pictures, the American photographer Eadweard Muybridge (1830–1904) was able to prove that suspension does indeed exist in the trot and the canter. This was the start of a revolution in gait analysis.

The Limited Human Eye

Readers of today's many richly illustrated horse publications might find it somewhat unbelievable that,

until 1878, generations of horse lovers debated the existence of "suspension." It is easy to discuss it now that we have seen countless pictures of Cocktail in the extended trot or Northern Dancer in a spectacular gallop. But, I'll argue that we should be less assuming and more conscious of the limitations of the human eye. You need to train your eye to notice specific characteristics when evaluating movement. For a more particular analysis, modern technology—which 100 years after Muybridge's discovery connected the film camera with the computer and introduced yet another revolution in the study of movement—is necessary. Current technology allows today's leading equine researchers (Fredricson, Holmström, Back, and Clayton, to name a few) to view the horse in full movement and, as a result, draw conclusions. This technology also allows me to make certain statements about the walk, trot, and canter in the remainder of this book.

The walk is a symmetrical gait: the movements of the left foreleg and hind leg form a mirror image of the movements of the right fore and hind leg. The hooves come into contact with the ground for equal amounts of time. Unlike the trot and canter, there is no period of suspension. The four legs overlap each other substantially during the "stance phase" (the period of time when the hoof is in contact with the ground).

Four Equal Parts

The walk is a four-beat gait: throughout one complete stride, the horse's four hooves come into contact with the ground individually. In a clean and *regular* walk, the placement of the legs can be divided into four equal parts, earmarked by the four moments of contact with

The American photographer, Eadweard Muybridge (1830–1904), proved the moment of suspension in the trot and gallop through his pioneering work in the nineteenth century.

the ground. In an *irregular* walk, the placement of the legs is less evenly distributed. If this irregularity increases, the result is a lateral gait where the left foreleg and hind leg, and the right foreleg and hind leg function as pairs.

The walk is a very difficult gait to judge with the human eye. There is a great deal of variation in the manner in which, as the FEI rule states, the "feet follow one another," mainly caused by significant differences in the time allowed for different stance phases of the legs. This was apparent in biomechanical evaluations of the horse on a treadmill. The horses had to walk and trot several times before they relaxed and researchers could attempt to make a correct judgment. The trot became consistent after three sessions, but some walk characteristics could not be reliably measured even after nine sessions. This shows us how observing and drawing corresponding conclusions about the walk

under studbook inspection circumstances is likely an inconsistent and questionable practice.

Footfall Regularity

In theory, what we should notice is the regularity of the footfalls that the walk divides into four equal parts. FEI rules express a great deal about the walk in **Article 403** but are somewhat ambiguous about the desired footfalls. **Paragraph 1:** *"The walk is a marching pace in which the footfalls of the horse's feet follow one another in 'four time,' well marked and maintained in all work at the walk."* In contrast, **Paragraph 2:** is very explicit about a deviation from the regularity described in **Paragraph 1:** *"This irregularity, which might become an ambling movement, is a serious deterioration of the pace."* Because of this FEI rule, some stallions, especially, have not been

approved for breeding purposes by the KWPN, regardless how attractive they may be otherwise.

FEI rules distinguish four types of walks, including the free walk (a relaxed pace where the horse is allowed to lower his head and stretch his neck):

Paragraph 4.1. The Collected Walk

"The hind legs are engaged with good hock action. The pace should remain marching and vigorous, the feet being placed in regular sequence. Each step covers less ground and is higher than at the medium walk, because all the joints bend more markedly. In order not to become hurried or irregular, the collected walk is shorter than the medium walk, although showing greater activity."

Paragraph 4.2. The Medium Walk

"A clear, regular and unconstrained walk of moderate lengthening...the hind feet touching the ground in front of the footprints of the forefeet."

Paragraph 4.3. The Extended Walk

"The horse covers as much ground as possible, without haste and without losing the regularity of his steps, the hind feet touching the ground clearly in front of the footprints of the forefeet."

There is considerable difference in the speed of each type of walk outlined by the FEI. In 1995, the equine biomechanics expert, Dr. Hilary Clayton, studied the walk of dressage horses and established that the average speed for the collected walk was 4.49 feet (1.37 meters) per second, while the average speed for the extended walk was 5.97 feet (1.82 meters) per second. Speed is the product of either stride frequency (the number of strides per minute) or stride length, or a combination of the two. Therefore, a horse can move faster by taking more strides, by taking longer strides, or by doing both. Clayton concluded in her study that the differences in speed between the types of walks outlined by the FEI was seldom due to an increase in stride frequency but instead largely caused by a lengthening of the strides, precisely as stipulated in the *FEI Rulebook*.

The Lateral Walk

Clayton's study yielded a remarkable discovery: only one out of six highly schooled dressage horses wholly fulfilled the criteria of a regular four-beat movement! This is remarkable but not quite unexpected. It is recognized that the laborious method of training often leads to a tightening through the horse's back. The tightening of the topline inhibits the movement of the hind legs, and this can produce a lateral gait in the walk. In addition, the FEI requires a great deal of lengthening in the walk stride (see p. 62). This favors selecting horses with "big" walks and, in the case of a horse with a far-reaching foreleg, the correct timing of the hind leg placement is often jeopardized.

Watch a young horse walking in the pasture, and you will rarely see a lateral walk (or a similar gait). This is a problem most often caused by incorrect training.

Limb Coordination

A four-beat movement certainly places higher demands on limb coordination than a two-beat gait (the trot) or a three-beat gait (the canter). Raising and setting down the four feet with perfect regularity places high demands on the coordination between the four individually moving limbs, which are each tied to the spinal cord. This coordination, then, is only possible if the back is supple and the rider does not interfere with the horse's use of it. The back easily becomes the first area to fall victim to bad training, making the walk a very significant gait to evaluate in the dressage arena. It proves whether or not the rider has followed the basic rules of the FEI regarding the correct development of the horse's "natural" characteristics.

Biomechanics researchers have already established a number of things about limb coordination, but I feel they should take a closer look at an aberration of the walk that appears at *least* as often as the lateral walk, and which I feel is certainly just as disturbing to the whole picture: the so-called "short-long" walk, which causes one hind leg to take a shorter step than the other hind leg. However, when the horse exhibiting the problem transitions to the trot he appears to move with total regularity. What causes this asymmetry of the hind legs in the walk? It is agreed that the most significant cause of the lateral walk is incorrect training, so should we then look for a physical cause for the short-long walk? While I am not sure of the answer, tension in the horse and lack of skill in the rider are likely culprits.

A "3" or a "10"

There is often a fine line between an incorrect and a brilliant walk (or, to use judging terms, a "3" or a "10"). Riders and trainers want that beautiful, big walk that they enjoy seeing so much—the one that can be collected with ease and regularity. However, it is completely unacceptable if that "beautiful, big walk" is combined with some inconsistency. What dressage horse breeders should do, then, is pinpoint the genetic components desired in the walk—regularity and length of stride—even if it means breeding horses that develop a lateral walk when they end up in the wrong hands.

It is very difficult to reliably measure the walk, even at a keuring.

ANKY VAN GRUNSVEN

Complete Calm and Immediate Relaxation

I think it's odd that the KWPN dismisses horses at keurings on the grounds they don't have a "pure" walk as incorrect walks are usually caused by poor riding, as mentioned in this chapter. (Besides, a keuring is certainly not a "natural" environment for the horse, so how can you judge what is natural for him?)

I didn't see the word "rhythm" in this chapter. I like a horse with an enthusiastic, active walk, which (to me) contains a "musical beat," so to speak. This kind of walk is rhythmic and easy to collect. A rider needs to have control of the walk because a horse can lose his rhythm if he isn't honestly forward; in other words, if he isn't sufficiently "in front of the leg." A horse can also lose his rhythm because his rider doesn't control his tempo well, letting him walk too slowly or too quickly. In these cases, the horse is always blamed for losing rhythm, but it is the rider's fault.

Analyzing the walk reveals how unbelievably difficult Grand Prix dressage is. It's hard enough getting a horse to piaffe, passage, and perform pirouettes, but then the horse also must demonstrate complete calm and instant relaxation after this kind of intense effort—and then be capable of immediately resuming the most difficult of movements! This is quite different from what happens in jumping, where there's one explosion of power that lasts two minutes. Dressage work consists of explosion and relaxation; explosion and relaxation; explosion and relaxation. It is logi-cal that the walk often pays the price for this kind of work, where two extremes are constantly balanced with one another.

The *FEI Rulebook* doesn't mention the *working* walk, which I find strange because I consider it the foundation of the gait. A young horse has to learn how to perform the working walk well before he can be taught the collected walk and medium walk.

My first Grand Prix horse, Prisco, walked short-long, which was a serious problem until we got our first hot walker. We did a lot of training with Prisco on the hot walker, equally in both directions, and that helped significantly. (The short-long walk can also certainly stem from rider error; for example, if a horse is locked up on one side.) I also did a lot of walk training with Bonfire. Bonfire's legs were always correct, but his problem was that he didn't show any "over-stride." We did cavalletti work; worked a lot on the circle in shoulder-fore and travers; and experimented with all kinds of other things. Bonfire began to work better through his body: he became looser and could lengthen his topline more, but the improvement over the ground was quite limited. He overstrided a little, sometimes a hoof's worth, but he never received more than a "6" for his walk.

The walk is a difficult gait—in contrast to the trot, the walk cannot be clearly improved. The most important thing for the rider to do is keep the walk pure.

The Trot: Hind Legs that "Accelerate" **13**

The transition from walk to trot is big: the horse goes from a four-beat gait without suspension to a two-beat gait with completely different characteristics. The trot has a relatively long moment of suspension (or one that can be lengthened, in any case), and the hooves contact the ground for a comparatively short period of time. Oddly, the back moves the least amount at the trot.

The trot shares one important similarity with the walk: both are symmetrical gaits. The movements of each foreleg mirror one another, and the same applies to hind legs.

The trot is also a diagonal gait: the left hind leg and right foreleg form a pair and vice versa. As mentioned before, the trot is a two-beat gait, so for each full stride, contact with the ground occurs twice. This, of course, has significant consequences for the distribution of weight: over and over again, 1,200 pounds (or more) rests on only two limbs and those two limbs' joints and tendons. In other words, the trot—and certainly the two-beat movements developed from the trot, namely the piaffe and passage—is a gait in which the horse is subjected to more stress and potential injury than the walk and, up to a certain point, the canter. (A fast canter can actually cause even greater stress.) Stress can be one reason for a horse to change his gait, as I mentioned earlier in this book. (Energy conservation and speed are the other reasons for a horse to change his gaits.)

If a horse wants to move faster than he is able to at the walk, then he must create a moment of suspension; otherwise, the length of his legs will limit the distance he can cover. Pole vaulters have to "thrust" themselves in order to clear a distance higher than the length of their pole, and horses have to do the same to go further than the length of their "poles," or in other words, their legs.

Stability

There is yet a fourth factor: stability. Every gait has its own rhythm, and it is with this that the horse maintains his balance. Maintaining balance in the four-beat walk is completely different than maintaining balance in the two-beat trot. In the walk, the considerable movement of the back coordinates the individually marching legs, and therefore makes equal weight distribution over the four legs possible. What occurs in the trot is not much different than the walk, except for the two-beat movement, which causes the back to act quite differently than it does in the walk. Whereas the walk requires continuous anticipation of the movements of each of the four legs, the trot has only take-off and landing of the diagonal pairs to worry about. So in contrast to the necessary movement of the back at the walk, the trot's diagonal physical balance and weight distribution requires the back to be held in a relatively stiff manner.

As in the last chapter, I will again refer to the *FEI Rulebook* for the different types of trot required in competitive dressage. You will see that one of the paragraphs I quote mentions the desire for the supple use of the back, which seems to contradict my point about the horse's limited use of his back in the trot. However, a less mobile back (as compared with the walk and the canter) can still be supple, and dressage riders know the feeling of a horse that "lets you sit" the trot, allowing the rider to "become one" with her mount.

Suppleness

The horse's ability to move "over his back"—despite the rider's additional weight—is developed through training. However, there are plenty of horses that are supple or stiff, depending on the day; that sometimes use their hind legs well and other times poorly; and that some days push more while other days less. Horses that consistently trot with impulsion and suppleness are easier to train and are a more comfortable ride. For this reason, it is good that the KWPN (NA/WPN) grades the apparent suppleness of a horse's trot on the Linear Score Sheet. (I will revisit the subject of suppleness in the next chapter when I discuss the combination of forward and upward movement.)

As with the walk, we want the horse to be able to considerably vary the length of his stride. In the previous chapter, we cited the work of Dr. Hilary Clayton, the biomechanics expert. Clayton established that, in elite dressage horses, the difference in speed between the different walks is mainly due to variation in stride length, not in stride frequency, which is precisely what the FEI likes to see. After all, dressage horses must maintain their rhythm, even when they go from a working gait to an extended gait.

Horses also prefer to trot at a specific frequency: whichever number of strides per minute is easiest for them. As stated, good dressage horses are able to create large differences in speed by varying the length of their trot strides. This suggests that the maximum lengthening of stride, and thus the maximum range in which variation can occur, is less in short-legged horses than in long-legged ones.

I would like to make one more comment before I go on: a recurring concept in the *FEI Rulebook* concerns impulsion from the hindquarters. The FEI clearly states time and again that the hindquarters must be active, stepping under the body; the weight from the forehand must be transferred to the hindquarters; and the hind legs must maintain impulsion.

According to FEI rules, a horse that is not yet trained in the collected exercises *must* eventually develop into a horse that can meet all the requirements regarding hindquarter activation.

Hind Legs that "Accelerate"

Dr. Hilary Clayton and her Swedish colleague Dr. Mikael Holmström have demonstrated the validity of the FEI rules. In two different experiments that took place in 1994 and 1997 respectively, they determined an essential phenomenon known as *Diagonal Advanced Placement* (DAP). In the natural movement pattern of the horse, the foreleg contacts the ground a fraction of a second earlier than its diagonal counterpart hind leg. The explanation of this phenomenon (which can only be seen with high-speed film cameras) is simple: the head and neck of the horse is heavier than his tail, and this unevenly balanced mass creates an accelerated placement of the foreleg. In contrast to this natural movement pattern, in the collected trot, well-trained (and talented) dressage horses can actually reverse the action and place their hind leg on the ground some 30 milliseconds before the diagonal foreleg.

Clayton and Holmström's experiments proved the obvious existence of a division of quality amongst dressage horses. Their work not only reinforced FEI rules but also encouraged a studbook that systematically selects horses for this desired use of the hind legs. The KWPN (NA/WPN) now clearly understands why it should select horses whose natural way of moving (on the forehand) can be manipulated by correct training and thus "accelerating" placement of the hind feet on the ground.

The Effects of Training

In 1995, Dr. Wim Back of Utrecht University, the Netherlands, studied the effects of dressage training. He observed that two-and-a-half-year-old horses that were actively being trained for dressage placed their hind legs farther under their bodies in the trot than they had prior to under saddle work. This increase in distance was in spite of the fact that these horses had originally been chosen for trots that already featured "maximum protraction" (extension forward) of the hind legs. After 70 days of training, these horses' hind legs had become stronger and quicker still.

In comparison, Back recorded the "performances" of horses the same age that were pastured twenty-four hours a day. These horses displayed slower, longer trot strides. The trained horses trotted with shorter strides, but this is likely because young horses just started under saddle are initially trying to find their balance and therefore have to place their feet on the ground relatively fast.

Back did a study a year before that revealed differences in the quality of dressage horses, in terms of movement, just as the Clayton study did. This study is of great interest to breeders because they want to distinguish good horses from bad ones in as objective a fashion as possible. Back's research focused on the movement traits of four-month-old foals, and then the same foals at twenty-six months. Professor Ab Barneveld, a very experienced and skilled judge of equine movement, provided subjective evaluations of each foal, which Back compared with objective measurements he took using "markers"—stickers glued to the foal's skin that precisely showed all aspects of the foal's movement when filmed.

The comparisons between good and fair-to-poor moving horses were so consistent that Back could name several objective indicators for a "good trot": maximum protraction of the *hind* legs, and *maximum retraction* of the *front* legs, resulting in a *long trot stride* with a *low stride frequency*. (These characteristics not only demonstrate power and balance; maximum protraction of the hind legs and maximum retraction of the front legs are also connected to a round and loose topline, as mentioned in chapter 9, p. 44.) In his research, Back also found that a relatively wide range of motion in the scapula and a great deal of fetlock joint extension are objective indicators of a good trot.

Article 404, Paragraph 3
"The quality of the trot is judged by the general impression,

the regularity and elasticity of the steps—originating from a supple back and well engaged hindquarters—and by the ability of maintaining the same rhythm and natural balance, even after a transition from one trot to another."

This rule evaluates whether—with respect to the moment of leg placement/hoof-ground contact—the trot strides are divided exactly into two halves. The elasticity of the strides is a separate issue, and we will further explore concepts such as impulsion and carrying power later in the book. Here, referencing biomechanical research that demonstrates the importance of accelerated diagonal placement of the hind legs is what matters. It proves that hindquarters that come well under the horse's body do make a difference when the horse is required to alter his natural tendency to carry weight on his forehand and transfer it to his hindquarters, a prerequisite for maintaining rhythm and balance as the tasks in the dressage arena grow more demanding. The rider can control the rhythm, movement, and balance of the horse by using his aids to steer the horse's hind legs.

The FEI distinguishes four types of trot: the collected trot, the working trot, the medium trot, and the extended trot.

4.1 The Collected Trot
"The hocks, being well engaged, maintain an energetic impulsion, thus enabling the shoulders to move with greater ease in any direction. The horse's steps are shorter than in the other trots, but he is lighter and more mobile."

With all due respect for the FEI, I have to disagree with the choice of words in the paragraph above. It is, of course, the hindquarters *in their entirety*, and not just the hocks, that maintain impulsion and provide the carrying power that enables the shoulders to move, not so much in "any" direction as simply back and forth. Furthermore, the elbows and knees (carpal joints) are much more responsible for the mobility of the front limbs than the shoulders are, which I will discuss further in the next chapter. I also feel the terms "lighter" and "mobile" should be explained in detail.

A good dressage horse's first—and most important— victory over Mother Nature is "accelerating" his hind leg placement, moving in a diagonal pairs and striding far under his body. Pictured here is Maaike Lassche on the KWPN stallion Parcival (Koss x Unitas), bred by A.J. Heijink.

As seen here, a horse's natural center of gravity is lower in the trot than when standing stationary. A dressage horse wastes a great deal of energy because his "upward" or elevated way of moving counters this lower center of gravity, and so he must defy Mother Nature a second time.

4.2 The Working Trot

"This is a pace between the collected and the medium trot, in which a horse, not yet trained and ready for collected movements, shows himself properly balanced and, remaining 'on the bit,' goes forward with even, elastic steps and good hock action. The expression 'good hock action'...only underlines the importance of an impulsion originating from the activity of the hindquarters."

4.3 The Medium Trot

"This is a pace between the working and the extended trot, but more 'round' than the latter. The horse goes forward with clear and moderately lengthened steps and with obvious impulsion from the hindquarters, always keeping the same character as in the working trot...The steps should be even, and the whole movement balanced and unconstrained."

The statements above are also not entirely clear. Many riders do not know what the word "round" means. Jan Peeters, an Olympic judge, informed me that "round" pertains to the horse's topline. The difference between an "elevated forehand" and "keeping the same character" needs to be clarified. Again, Jan Peeters explained that "keeping the same character" refers to the horse's head-and-neck position and the contact, while "an elevated forehand" pertains to the perceived direction of the horse's body.

In any case, a horse must show a certain degree of elevation in his entire body in each of the different types of trot, the maximum is required in the collected trot and the minimum is required in the extended trot when the horse lengthens his body and his legs the most.

Center of Gravity

The elevated forehand desired by the FEI is the second example of a good dressage horse's ability to defy the laws of nature, a feat we first acknowledged with the example of changing diagonal leg placement timing (see p. ooo). The same concept of "going against nature" applies to maintaining an elevated forehand in the trot.

During the trot, the horse's center of gravity is naturally lower than when he is standing stationary and square. Look at Standardbred trotters, for example. They get extremely close to the ground during their spectacular acceleration. The lower center of gravity makes the trot an energy-conserving gait. Dressage horses must do exactly the opposite of what trotters do: they make themselves "bigger," or "higher" than when they are standing still. Moving against gravity in this manner requires more energy.

Both of the dressage horse's "victories" over Mother Nature have a great deal to do with one another: only hind legs that can "accelerate" and step far under the body enable a horse to move with an elevated forehand.

4.4 The Extended Trot

"The horse covers as much ground as possible. Maintaining the same cadence, he lengthens his steps to the utmost as a result of great impulsion from the hindquarters...The forefeet should touch the ground on the spot towards which they are pointing. The movement of the fore and hind legs should be similar (parallel) in the forward moment of the extension. The whole movement should be well balanced and the transition to collected trot should be smoothly executed by taking more weight on the hindquarters."

If the rider uses too much hand and asks the horse for too much extension in the trot, the result is not only a tight back, but tightness in every aspect of the movement—in particular, the horse holds his front legs stiffly. When this occurs, the suppleness necessary for the horse to bend his knees—and thus fulfill the requirement of the front feet landing on the spots at which they point—disappears. Farbenfroh used to occasionally show a very extreme form of the extended trot. The quest for length of stride came at the cost of the calm and suppleness needed for him to pick up his knees and release them, or "set them down," and his front feet would have had to land on the moon in order to fulfill the FEI requirements!

Cannons and Soldiers

"The movement of the fore and hind legs should be similar (parallel) in the forward moment of the extension." This wording needs some explanation: in other words, the extended trot must be performed equally by both the front and hind legs: "cannons will only boom if soldiers fire them from behind."

ANKY VAN GRUNSVEN

Talent is the Most Important Consideration

I use the trot to make horses elastic; I use it to gymnasticize them. It's also the gait a rider can make the most of, provided that the horse has the ability. Bonfire, of course, is a great example of this. I like horses that you can take from a "pony trot" to a spectacular extended trot, and everything in between. And, I don't mind teaching them how to do it.

I don't like horses that *always* show a spectacular trot. A horse simply can't keep that up, and it makes collection, in particular, more difficult. There are very few horses that can do a perfect extended trot as well as a perfect piaffe or passage. Even among the top horses in the world you see that one has more trouble with extensions, and another has more trouble with piaffe and passage. Competitive dressage, to a great extent, is about training (and what I stated above about the "adjustable" trot still holds true), but ultimately at Grand Prix level, natural talent is the most important consideration.

Everything in this chapter about the hind legs is true. I always deal with the hind legs first because if you want to achieve something in competitive dressage, that's where it begins.

A horse that doesn't move his back much is very comfortable to ride, but that's not what you look for in a dressage horse. My best horses were initially not the easiest ones to sit the trot on, precisely because of the way they used their backs. Everything happened underneath me, and I liked that. And, training eventually made sitting the trot on those horses very nice as they became balanced.

It certainly might be true that trot work imposes the most stress on a horse's legs, but personally, if I'm starting a horse back to work after an injury, I use the trot. I think the trot is actually less stressful in a way because the strides are more evenly distributed over two legs, while the canter, for example, puts too much stress on one leg.

I agree that the *FEI Rulebook* sometimes needs some clarification. "Lighter," "mobile," "rounder"—what do you do with these words? The clearer they can make the description, the less room there is for debate when it comes to judging.

The Canter: The FEI and Mother Nature Conflict

14

A dressage horse's fastest gait is not the same as the horse's fastest "natural" gait. The canter, required in dressage tests, occurs at speeds up to 36 feet (11 meters) per second. Horses can, however, reach much higher speeds, and the gait used is substantially different from the "dressage canter."

The English language makes a clear distinction: the word "canter" applies to the gait used in dressage and the word "gallop" to the horse's fastest gait. The difference between these two gaits is an extra individual moment of contact with the ground. The canter has three beats; the gallop has four.

Throughout this chapter, my discussion concerns the three-beat gait prescribed by the FEI. The following description of the *four-beat canter* does *not* refer to the high speed gallop in which the horse lengthens his body, facilitating the fourth moment of contact with the ground—in other words, the process that occurs on the racetrack. Instead, the four-beat canter is a deviant and undesired gait that, according to FEI rules, must be scored as "insufficient."

The Four-Beat Canter

It is common to see dressage horses slip into a four-beat canter as a result of less speed: in turns, on circles, in the half-pass, and in collection prior to a pirouette. This has nothing to do with the natural four-beat motion of the gallop.

Earlier, I discussed how the human eye limits our ability to thoroughly analyze a horse's movement. We can do our best to grasp the most important aspects of equine movement and train our eye to select for the essential traits. The difference between a correct three-beat canter and an incorrect four-beat canter is among

these traits, and it happens to be one judges tend to notice quite easily!

As previously determined for the walk and the trot, a gait cannot be viewed only in terms of related leg movement. The horse's legs are each in direct contact with the back, and raising the limbs and moving them forward and backward directly affects the back's mobility. The three-beat canter creates a very mobile back, and because of suspension—which also can be called "jump" because there is a "point of takeoff"—it is a gait with a clear vertical motion.

Just as with the walk and the trot, the canter must be both collected and extended in dressage tests. When extending, the dressage horse (unlike his racetrack counterparts) is not allowed to lengthen his body, which would bring his body closer to the ground. In contrast, an extended canter requires more elevation to enable the horse to increase the size of his strides.

A Working Relationship

How do the horse's legs move in the canter? The front legs work together; the hind legs work together; and the two pairs must maintain a relationship with each other. In contrast to the walk and trot, the canter is an asymmetrical gait: the movement of the two front legs and two hind legs do not mirror one another. In each stride, both the front leg pair and the hind leg pair feature one leg set farther forward. The leg that is farthest forward is called the *leading leg*, and the other leg in each pair is called the *trailing leg*.

The working relationship between the leading and the trailing leg—for both the front and the hind legs—is based on a distribution of functions: the leading leg reaches the farthest forward and is capable of the greatest range of motion; the trailing leg stores the most energy and thus contributes the most to an elastic and energy-conserving gait. In

1995, Dr. Marianne M. Sloet van Oldruitenborgh-Oosterbaan from the Faculty of Veterinary Medicine at Utrecht University, the Netherlands, established that the fetlock joints of the trailing legs extend more, which loads the flexor tendons of these legs with more "passive energy," a stress that is then released in the subsequent "takeoff."

Leg Placement

The footfall sequence in the canter is as follows: trailing hind leg followed by simultaneous contact of the diagonal pair consisting of the leading hind leg and trailing front leg; then the leading front leg touches the ground, followed by a period of suspension. So, in a right-lead canter, this equates to: the left hind leg, followed by the right hind and the left front leg (simultaneously), the right front leg, and then the period of suspension. The highly undesirable four-beat canter is caused by the uncoupling of the diagonal pair, and the sequence then becomes: trailing hind leg, leading hind leg, trailing front leg, leading front leg, and then the period of suspension.

The period of suspension can help you evaluate the quality of a horse's canter. A horse with a four-beat canter will display a limited period of suspension. Horses with a good canter not only have a clear three-beat gait but also a pronounced period of suspension that can actually be seen as the "jump" I mentioned earlier. This "jump" is necessary to eventually performing a technically correct flying change.

The flying change takes place during the period of suspension, initiated by the hind leg and executed both in front and behind simultaneously. This is in contrast to racehorses that first change in front, followed by behind.

A Serious Conflict

In chapter 13, I explained that at the trot the horse must twice defy the laws of nature. In the canter, a serious conflict exists in the canter between the FEI and Mother Nature. The FEI requires extreme collection, even a movement in the same spot (the pirouette) in the gait that the horse would naturally choose to move faster and travel more distance. It is, therefore, easy to understand why problems arise when shortening the canter stride. FEI rules include the following in regards to maintaining the three-beat rhythm:

Article 405, Paragraph 3

"The quality of the canter is judged by the general impression, the regularity and lightness of the three time pace...and by the ability of maintaining the same rhythm and natural balance, even after a transition from one canter to another."

During collected canter work, the hindquarters must lower and accept a great deal of the horse's body weight, which naturally falls on the forehand. At the same time, the moving horse must distribute his body weight over his four legs so there are no gait irregularities. All of these complex factors mutually affect one another: carrying weight on the hindquarters, maintaining balance, and coordinating leg placement—all by way of a supple back. Obviously, a great deal can go wrong in this complex equation and is often betrayed by a four-beat gait.

A lack of power or balance can lead to a four-beat canter. In addition, tension in the horse's topline can cause the uncoupling of the diagonal pair of legs. Both the horse's back coordination and the rider's influence (specifically, the rider's hands) impact gait regularity. On the other hand, the training process may lead to a combination of these factors. It can be a vicious circle: because a horse has more difficulty establishing carrying power or balance, a rider does more with his body and hands, which subsequently only further disturbs the action of the horse's back and the regularity of movement. I feel that researchers who specialize in biomechanics need to again address the relationship between the horse's use of his hind legs, the distribution of his weight, and the loss of gait regularity.

"Trotters" versus "Racehorses"

In a previous chapter about the dressage horse's movement, we established that the *similarities* between the three basic gaits are greater than the *differences*. This remains true. However, there *are* substantial differences, and the difference in the trot and canter is when "talent" is the most evident. We have clearly identified groups of horses that show incredible push, power, and length of stride in the trot but must exert much more effort than other horses to maintain a three-beat canter, particularly when they have to do something other than canter forward and straight ahead. Likewise, there are other groups of horses that have to learn how to extend the trot but can maintain their canter rhythm in almost any situation and, therefore, also have far less difficulty with collection and movement in the canter. Researchers specializing in biomechanics should also further study the traits of these different types of dressage horses.

As with the walk and the trot, the canter must show a great degree of variation in the length of stride, according to FEI rules.

Article 405, Paragraph 4.3 The Medium Canter

"The horse goes forward with free, balanced and moderately extended strides and an obvious impulsion from the hindquarters."

4.4 The Extended Canter

"Maintaining the same rhythm, he lengthens his strides to the utmost…"

We established earlier that good dressage horses are capable of extending or collecting while only minimally changing their stride frequency. In other words, we can see differences in quality between horses by noting their ability to lengthen without quickening their strides. We also see differences in quality with the opposite exercise: when the horse must achieve extreme collection, for example, in the pirouette, he may tend to decrease the frequency of his canter strides. In this particular exercise, eight canter strides obviously require much more strength than five canter strides, and a decrease in canter stride frequency indicates a lack of carrying power. This phenomenon appears just as often in the other basic gaits. It affects upward and forward movement, which we will discuss further in the next chapter. Below is another essential passage from the FEI Rulebook concerning the canter:

Article 405, Paragraph 2 The Canter

"The canter, always with light, cadenced and regular strides, should be moved into without hesitation."

It is interesting to notice that the FEI has only mentioned the importance of a canter depart without hesitation, though a variation in quality between the first trot strides (or the first strides in the walk) with those that follow is also undesirable. Normally, this demonstrates that a particular horse needs tempo to remain in balance. The horse that moves in balance from the very first stride naturally has more dressage ability—a sport that puts balance, especially, to the test—than a horse that needs time to find his balance.

We conclude this chapter by saying, once again, that every stride begins from the horse's hind end, and specifically, his hind legs.

ANKY VAN GRUNSVEN

Keeping the Horse Forward

The canter is the gait we can use—more so than the trot—to develop a horse's power. Riding horses is about variation. You don't make a horse strong and give him stamina by riding the canter alone, but in addition to other exercises, the canter is very useful for this purpose.

In dressage, the further along in training the horse is, the more important the canter becomes. Grand Prix contains more movements in the canter than in the trot. Therefore, we need to impose very high standards for the canter at Grand Prix level.

In collection, it is true that many problems crop up with rhythm and tempo. Horses are ridden "backward": they slow down instead of collecting, or they lose the correct three-beat canter. The main characteristic of good collection is a forward feel in the canter with lots of push. Variation is also a good aid for maintaining rhythm. Varying the tempo teaches a horse to keep his balance.

The sections in this chapter that discuss speed in the canter and teaching collection are certainly correct. A young horse needs time. This is why we initially do a lot of training on the 20-meter circle. However, a talented horse, one that naturally lets you close up his stride and one that lowers his hindquarters will easily learn to collect and enjoy it.

Krack C in the extended canter. Since a dressage horse must not lengthen his body, he has to "jump" higher to be able to lengthen his strides to their maximum. Krack C "jumped" so high at the World Cup in Jerez, Spain, that his rider was partially cut out of the picture!

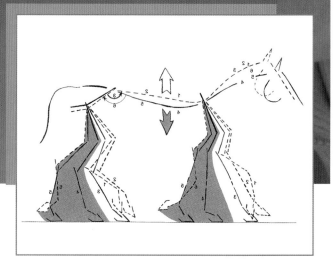

We cannot evaluate gaits only in terms of the horse's leg movement. Because a horse's legs are in direct contact with his back, raising his limbs and moving them forward and backward directly affects the mobility of the spinal column. Here, the numbers indicate corresponding periods of movement.

Comparing Roman and Gothic Churches

15

We have discussed the technical aspects of the three basic gaits. We have also looked at the three different types of leg movement and their effect on the spinal column. However, these things do not tell us everything about the quality of a dressage prospect's basic gaits.

A dressage horse meets the FEI's first requirement if he moves around the arena in a nice four-beat, two-beat, and three-beat rhythm, respectively, but this is not enough to make a horse a world champion. If a horse moves without expression, without hind legs that naturally carry, without collection, and with little suppleness, judges will ultimately not be impressed, and horse and rider will receive low scores.

Dressage is primarily about showing off a horse's optimal movement, but it is not a pleasure class. "Something" has to happen in movement, and it has to look beautiful and easy (on both the rider and horse's part!)

Upward Movement

A dressage horse must do more than just maintain his rhythm in the various gaits. He must also add value by being more than just beautiful. This chapter discusses this concept of "added value." We will look at a dressage horse's ability to move forward and, in particular, to move *upward*.

The movement of a horse's limbs is comparable to the doors and windows of an old church. A church has a foundation and a peak, and the peak is always located in the center of the foundation. The foundation can be broad, like that of a Roman church (a horse that moves with very big strides). On the other hand, a church can be narrow with a relatively high peak, which is more a Gothic style (a horse that moves with elevation and collection). Good dressage horses (that are also well trained) can demonstrate both the Roman style (big strides) and the Gothic style (vertical strides) in one dressage test. Furthermore, they can also bend their hind legs in an arch under their bodies to a greater or lesser extent, depending on the required movement.

The evaluation of movement has traditionally favored big strides. Breeders now know that we have to look at movement in a different way. The vertical (upward) component is probably more important than the horizontal (forward) one—and both are genetic.

A carriage horse, for example, is selected strictly for his vertical movement: his "show trot." If we let a carriage horse canter loose, we can see that this vertical movement desired at the trot also expresses itself with a distinctive—but not so desirable—"stamping" canter. This obviously doesn't suggest that the carriage horse type should occupy a place in dressage horse breeding, but it does show that vertical movement can be improved through careful selection.

Björsell's Briar

A less extreme example than the carriage horse mentioned above, and one more relevant to dressage, is Björsell's Briar, the Swedish Grand Prix stallion that was required to gallop a certain distance around a track during his performance test.

At the time, the young stallion moved forward

Pays Bas NL (Cabochon x Zeoliet), ridden by Christa Laarakkers, demonstrates the expression desired in the front legs at the trot and canter. Pays Bas NL's breeder and co-owner is Gert Willem van Norel.

around the track in an uneconomical, frantic, and undoubtedly very fatiguing way, but at the same time demonstrated tremendous talent for vertical dressage movement. Currently, Björsell's Briar is a successful Grand Prix horse that can perform an exemplary piaffe, transition into the canter, and flow directly into a pirouette—and easily repeat the exercise in the reverse order without missing a stride! This horse's talent for vertical movement enables him to connect these exercises without visible effort.

Characteristics of vertical movement include quick "folding" or flexing of the hind legs (decreasing and increasing the angles of the hind legs quickly and to a great extent), and an expressive knee action (bending of the knees).

If we want to create a relationship—a link—between talented young dressage horses and the top of the sport, we have to value traits such as flexion in the joints, even if stride length is not optimum. Because suspension exists in the trot and canter and training can strengthen the hind legs, we can improve horizontal movement over time; in contrast, vertical movement depends mainly on talent, which we can only improve through breeding selection.

Eohippus

It is wise to reflect back on the "horse" that has evolved over millions of years through a long series of adaptations. Eohippus, the sluggish, rummaging, forest dweller, had four toes and was no bigger than a dog. It has taken 55 million years to transform Eohippus into a single-hoofed athlete that dances in a 20 x 60 meter arena. Now, the horse is approximately 16.3 hands tall with the ability to reach high speeds and exhibit great stamina. However, what is most important to us is that the horse is suitable for a sport in which suppleness, rhythmic movements, and grace are paramount.

Inertia

What happens when a horse rhythmically dances in a coordinated, swinging, forward-and-upward direc-

tion? With relatively little effort, a forward "swing" can be maintained in the upper legs; this impulsion slows down almost immediately but is enough to move the limbs forward and thus "launch" the hooves. As a result of inertia (the hoof's natural resistance to a change in velocity), the hoof shoots forward, creating a big stride with a minimal amount of muscular effort. This phenomenon perpetuates a very efficient manner of moving, which due to the length and relatively low weight of the horse's lower limbs, is unsurpassed in the animal kingdom.

Elastic Energy

Upon each stride's landing, the horse stores some of the downward gravitational force in his tendons and joints. This energy is then released like a spring in the second part of the stride phase, when the horse takes off again. In this way, the joints and tendons act as shock absorbers and, to a certain extent, transform *kinetic energy* (the energy that the horse's body needs to move from rest to a certain velocity, or from one speed to another) into *elastic energy* (the energy that the horse's moving body produces when it is moved from its original resting position—similar to the energy created when a spring is depressed, and then released), and vice versa.

Most of us have no idea such efficiency and conservation of energy takes place before our eyes each day! We can certainly see the difference between a horse moving with elasticity and one resembling a block of wood. Suppleness is not only expressed in vertical movement; consider the way a horse bends easily around a rider's leg. However, we actually see a great deal of the horse's natural suppleness in his up-and-down movement—the processing and use of kinetic energy, and optimal spring upward after every landing. These things are all "suppleness," and we attribute a significant part of the perceived quality of a horse's movement to it.

Keeping the Frequency Low

The movement as described above serves a function: it

keeps the number of strides to a minimum while increasing their length, a quality constantly endorsed by the FEI. An increase in kinetic energy as a result of increased speed is due to the suppleness of the tendons that absorb and assimilate the escalated impact caused by extension. (A stiff horse, one with reduced capacity for storing elastic energy, must increase his stride frequency in order to accommodate an increase in kinetic energy.) Something similar applies to the reverse effect: a horse is able to maintain stride frequency in the piaffe and passage while barely moving forward because the soft tissue around the pasterns can act as flexible "springs" (a phenomenon incorrectly called "pastern elasticity" by some). Therefore, the natural suppleness of the dressage horse works in both extension and collection, helping to maintain cadence, regularity, and rhythm.

Our Eyes Trick Us

Let us look more closely at what the different parts of the horse's limbs do in motion, beginning with the front legs. Traditionally, shoulder freedom was viewed as the quality that distinguished good movers from average movers, at least with respect to the use of the front legs. However, movement analysis using modern cameras has demonstrated that our eyes have tricked us all along. In 1994, Dr. Mikael Holmström discovered that the most important difference between good and poor use of the front legs was the horse's use of the elbow and the knee (carpal) joint, with the elbow being the most important. Unfortunately, the naked human eye is unable to see that the elbow joint has approximately 30 degrees more forward movement in horses with good movement as opposed to those with

The horse's joints and tendons serve to both absorb shock and transform kinetic energy into elastic energy.

"Vertical" movement consists of the hind legs "folding" (the angle between the cannon and gaskin closing) cleanly and quickly, and the fore-arms lifting higher to allow more bend in the knees.

poor movement. In these same horses, the shoulder revealed only a slight difference. As a result of this extra space for movement in the elbow joints, the horse lifts his front legs higher, which enables him to bend his knees more and then move/swing each front leg farther forward—the "knee action" that dressage riders so like to see.

Maximum Variation

The desired movement of the joints described earlier in this chapter allows horses to better fulfill the FEI's requirement for maximum variation of stride length and placement of the front feet on "the ground on the spot towards which they are pointing," as described in **Article 404, paragraph 4.4** Let me express this in breeding terms: a horse can better finish his forehand stride with more space for movement in the elbow joint. This characteristic also relates to the desirable long upper arm because a longer upper arm facilitates a longer triceps muscle, which in turn, is important for bending the elbow joint.

If we turn our attention to the movement of the hind legs, then we will see that the hip joint appears to move the least of all the hind joints. This is indeed true because the hip joint actually moves 10 degrees less

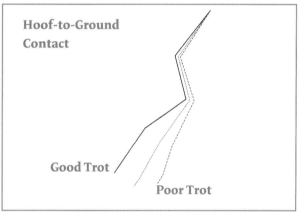

The angles of the front leg when in the forward-most position in movement: It can be seen here that the amount of room for movement in the elbow makes the difference between a good trot and a poor trot.

than the hock and the stifle joints do. We also miss an important part of the hip joint's movement as the thigh bone (femur) slides beneath the skin, thus concealing the action. This contrasts with the movements of the other joints, which are visible to the naked eye.

Equal Bend

The stifle and hock joints work equally in degrees of timing and amount of bend (Wentink, 1978). These are joints

ANKY VAN GRUNSVEN

Expression

Everything in this chapter is certainly true. I found reading about the elbow's important role and the other physiological points to be educational; however, I'm a practical person, and I say that we can indeed see the difference between good and poor moving horses. It doesn't matter whether you use the term "shoulder freedom" or "elbow use," as long as we all agree about what is and isn't desirable in a horse's movement. What's more, I don't use the words "shoulder freedom" as often as I use "knee action." I look at how expressive a horse is when he moves, and the way he completes his strides. Knee action is an important part of this, and I completely agree with the concept that a horse can only move with expression and "far-reaching" front legs if he uses his elbow well to lift them.

Horses that move with big, forward strides versus those that move with collected and upward strides, have been discussed before. I continue to think that, by and large, most horses are either Gothic movers or Roman movers—one rarely comes across a world-class horse that moves in both styles equally well.

Dressage riders look for "elastic" horses, and a large part of that suppleness does indeed come from flexing in the fetlocks and pasterns. I think Bonfire is a model of "elasticity": when he piaffed and passaged, his pasterns were almost on the ground. Bonfire's pasterns are sufficiently long, which is necessary for suppleness, but *too* long is definitely *not* good. Suppleness must not become a weakness.

that are reciprocally bound to one another. Furthermore, they bend mainly because of the release of elastic energy, which is relative to the amount a horse moves "off the ground" and "recharges" with kinetic energy as a result of speed and gravity (see p. 77). The simultaneous coupling of both the extension and contraction of these joints is a characteristic specific to the hind leg. Dr. G.H. Wentink (the Netherlands) demonstrated that the bend of the hock and pastern joints are linked during suspension, as well. The moment of maximum flexion of the hock (and, therefore, also the stifle) within the period of suspension corresponds with the maximum flexion of the pastern joints.

By addressing the elasticity of the horse's vertical movement, the true quality of the horse's overall movement is partially unveiled. The *extension* and *contraction* of the joints is important to this elasticity, which will become more apparent when we address the relationship between upward and forward movement as well as collection.

"Hay-Balers" and Turbo Horses **16**

The previous chapter included the ambiguous statement: "Something has to happen in movement." What is that "something"? If we could sum up that "something" with one word, it would be "collection."

A horse must collect when performing specific high school exercises, as well as when he simply does "regular" dressage—or at least, a working horse's natural movement pattern should alter through steady contact and the rider's activating aids. The horse should no longer move long and flat (his natural way of conserving energy); instead, his topline should round and he should move with more elevation. Then, the foundation for true collection has been laid.

Until recently, FEI dressage riders were instructed to improve the horse's *natural* qualities. However, is that really what we are doing if we teach a horse to transfer weight to his hindquarters? Experts have argued that horses can naturally perform piaffe, passage, and pirouettes—just look at the impressive behavior of a stallion parading in his pasture. If that is the case, the only thing a rider should have to do is put a saddle on the horse and "find" this natural talent!

Natural Movement Characteristics

The reality is we train dressage horses to move so that they sometimes carry more than half their weight on their hindquarters instead of their forehand. We can hardly call this state "natural"; however, it is not completely unnatural, either, because the only tools we have are our hands, legs, time, sweat, and soul—and of course, our horse's natural capabilities.

One thing must be realized: whether or not this carriage is natural, it only applies when the horse is in motion. As soon as the horse stands still, he once again carries 60 percent of his weight on the forehand. It is primarily the natural *movement* characteristics of the dressage horse that help transfer his weight to his hindquarters.

In the previous chapter, we discussed natural movement qualities that have been applied to dressage and resulted in exceptional beauty. Inertia enables a horse to move efficiently, but also contributes to an incredible reach in the extended trot. Elastic energy also contributes to a horse's efficient and unique ability to conserve energy, but we are only conscious of it when a horse engages in an extravagant exercise, such as the passage or piaffe.

Use of the Hind Legs

In chapter 13 (see p. 65) we discussed the major quality differences between elite dressage horses and ordinary horses. These differences seemed to be primarily associated with the timing of the horse's hind leg placement. Good dressage horses, with training, have a natural ability to place one hind foot on the ground a fraction of a second sooner than the diagonal-paired front foot. This phenomenon is only possible if the hindquarters are lowered, relative to the forehand. Such a body position is in turn connected to the hindquarters being capable of accepting weight. There are, of course, differences between horses in the natural way they use their hind legs. We have all seen the "hay-balers" (horses that appear to be kicking out toward their tails with every step of their hind legs);

This horse has not placed his hind leg far enough under his body. He does not show sufficient elevation, and his croup is too high.

and we have also seen the "turbo horses" that place their hind legs so far forward under their bodies as to be remarkable. The dressage horse breeder looks for the latter: horses with a powerful "motor" behind.

Quick to React

The ability to place the hind foot on the ground a fraction sooner than the diagonal front foot has been scientifically demonstrated in the trot; however, there is no reason to assume that this "hind leg acceleration" is limited to the trot. A horse must carry himself in every gait and in every exercise. This helps regulate his balance and has everything to do with the reflex speed of the hind legs. In other words, breeders do not look for horses that can just bring their hind legs under their body well—they must quickly react to impulses and changes and develop activity in their joints.

Regardless if one is a person or an animal, movement always consists of both a *vertical* and a *horizontal* component. You must first pick up your leg before you can move it forward. Nature has determined a specific

ideal relationship between this upward and forward motion for every horse. As I mentioned earlier in this book, Mother Nature has given the horse several reasons for not deviating too much from this ideal balance. If a horse loses this balance, then—under natural circumstances—he simply changes gaits.

Speed and Stride Rhythm

Dressage performance requires that the natural relationship between the horse's upward and forward movement change via training, giving the horse the ability to adjust his stride speed and rhythm when asked by his rider. In the collected gaits and exercises in place (such as the piaffe), speed decreases while the stride rhythm remains the same. This assumes the upward movement of the limbs remains the same while the stride length gradually decreases to zero. (According to the FEI, the upward movement should actually increase in the collected gaits because they should be more active and elevated than the extensions!)

Let us look more carefully at what the hind leg actu-

This horse's right hind leg demonstrates a very functional "arch" brought well under his body, and the horse shows carrying power, as well.

ally does when the horse is in motion. The hind leg of a coldblooded (draft) horse, for example, is lifted almost vertical and put down again very quickly—especially when pulling a heavy tree trunk. The hind legs are not brought forward underneath his body. A coldblooded horse should not possess elevated gaits, and he certainly need not move with self-carriage. He is bred for his body to do one thing: push forward with strength and efficiency.

If we use the metaphor from the previous chapter, the coldblooded horse's hind leg movement is Gothic church-style: the peak is higher than the width of the foundation. And, this "arched" movement occurs somewhere in the area beneath his docked tail. Dressage horses, in contrast, must display movement that features the "arch" of the hind leg further forward and underneath their bodies, rather than their tails.

Structural Blockage

How is it possible that some horses—even those with the most "heart" in the world—cannot place their hind legs sufficiently under their bodies? Perhaps both horse and rider try to the best of their ability, but something stands in the way. Aside from rider error, several different things can cause this problem.

When we addressed the conformation of the horse, I described several potential structural shortcomings. For example, a horse that is built with relatively long hind legs and relatively short front legs obviously has to put more effort into transferring weight onto his hindquarters when in motion than a horse that is naturally built uphill. However, we sometimes find a horse with ideal conformation that still moves around the arena like a pony, and there are also horses built on the forehand that move like athletes and place their hind legs well underneath their body. This proves once again that we cannot judge a horse until we have seen him in motion. Above all, we can rightfully conclude that the horse's natural carriage—Point 2, "Body: Direction," on the KWPN (NA/WPN) Linear Score Sheet—is simply a guideline for potential dressage ability, and does not necessarily dictate a prospect's future success.

A good dressage horse should place his hind legs as far under his body as possible. A horse may not be able to do this because of either physical or psychological factors, or both.

Many researchers have demonstrated the negative influence of a straight femur. This is logical, for this bone connects the hip joint and the stifle joint, and if it is positioned more or less perpendicular to the hip joint (straight), it places the entire hind leg behind the body. As a result, the horse literally moves against a physical "blockage" when he brings his hind legs forward. The hind leg has sufficient vertical movement but insufficient forward movement. A hay-baling machine, which throws hay bales up into the air and onto the ground behind it is a good metaphor for this pattern of movement. The equine journalist, Henk Bouwman (the Netherlands), first made this comparison.

Hind Leg Use and Temperament

In this book, when we discuss the dressage horse's temperament, our conclusions are based on a survey of 700 riders (246 respondents) who are members of the Dutch ZZGP Foundation (competitors at 4th level and higher), in the hope that we can perhaps determine the value of a horse with a good attitude and a diligent work ethic. A horse reveals his temperament by the way he moves as well as the way he behaves. If we were to compare a group of horses that use their hind legs well with a group of horses that use their hind legs poorly, those in the first group might appear to have more "energetic" temperaments than those in the second group. Of all the aspects of a dressage horse, I find this gray, interactive area between body and soul is the most intriguing.

In Part Three of this book, entitled "Temperament," we will see if our survey can further illuminate this subject.

Collection, of course, is largely dependant on the hind legs. However, collection (or its preparatory training, in any case) has a significant effect on the front legs. The general consensus among those in the horse industry is that a horse in collection carries himself on his hind legs,

A N K Y   V A N   G R U N S V E N

Not without Lightness!

I consider a "quick reaction time" to be one of the most important qualities in a dressage horse. A horse must be alert—to the leg, to collection, and to the rein aids. There are plenty of horses that are "good movers," with power and big strides. However, if a horse does not quickly react, then you can never get him to work to his full potential, certainly where collection is concerned. This kind of horse tends to get crabby, and is certainly not the "happy athlete" we like to see.

It's incredibly important in the collected movements to maintain a horse's desire to move forward. The *speed* of the forward movement in passage and piaffe indeed decreases, but the horse's *desire* to move forward must remain undiminished. Even at the halt, a horse must still think "forward"; otherwise, you won't be able to remotivate the hind legs. There's no impulsion without the desire to move forward!

Collection does improve front leg action, but I think that the quality of the front legs mainly has to do with a horse's natural ability and rider contact. This chapter discusses "steady" contact, but I'd like to change that to "steady, *light* contact." You see horses get tight in their front legs if they're "ridden with the hand." Some riders "hold" their horses in piaffe and then complain about the lack of expression in the horse's front legs.

I'd also like to comment on the claim that "with the...lowering of the hindquarters, the hind legs move further underneath the body." The hind legs must not extend too far under the body. In piaffe, it regularly happens that a horse suddenly moves his hind legs too far under his body (which is a faulty transition) and then can no longer perform the exercise in an acceptable manner. The biggest challenge in collection is really how magnanimous we expect the horse to be in his work. Of course, we want collection—but not without lightness! This magnanimity is very much connected with the temperament, attitude, and the natural forward desire that distinguishes a top dressage horse from an ordinary one.

thus lightening his forehand. It is true that the hind legs become more active in collection and push more off the ground, but the same applies to the front legs: they elevate the front part of the horse, raising his forehand above his hindquarters.

We discovered in the previous chapter that the elbow joints serve the most important function for the front legs, but increasing impulsion from the hindquarters (which is connected to maintaining elevation and lengthening the moment of suspension) also supports the forward extension of the front legs.

An important role exists for the front legs, even when performing very collected exercises like the piaffe and passage: they have to give expression to the movement. Some horses that actually lack the power in their hind legs necessary to perform a correct piaffe nonetheless appear capable because of the lift and natural expression in their front legs.

Collection

Let's look at collection in the stricter sense of the word. What happens if a horse, while retaining his rhythm and regularity and constantly moving forward on the bit, has to move with "small" strides? Let's look at this in the steps the horse's body will go through:

1. Transfer of body weight to the hindquarters by quickly placing the hind legs under or passed the horse's center of gravity.

2. Lower the hindquarters by tilting the pelvis. (This process begins in the topline because the horse's spinal cord is of solid construction.) The pelvic area must tilt to introduce (and participate in) the lowering of the hindquarters. The muscle group responsible for the tilting is hidden in the pelvic cavity (see p. 46).

3. Reduce the angles in the hind legs. This augments the lowering of the hindquarters.

4. Concurrent with the reduction of the angles and the lowering of the hindquarters, the hind legs move further underneath the body, whereby a part of the support function must be taken over by muscle power. The elevation of the forehand, in turn, causes the weight to shift to the hindquarters.

5. The activity of the hindquarters increases relative to the reduction of speed, depending on the degree of collection required. The continuous upward movement, while the horse remains almost static, puts extra strain on the horse's muscle power and his ability to remain in balance.

Collection, therefore, requires extreme power. The potential for this power can be observed in a talented young horse in the way he uses his hind legs: under his body, with a great deal of bend and thrust, and with the capacity for lightning-quick tempo changes while maintaining his balance. These are all characteristics that are closely scrutinized during movement evaluations at KWPN (NA/WPN) selections.

Despite these evaluations, a young horse's true capacity for collection is not yet present. This power slowly develops from a foundation of talent by adding ingredients like time, training, and determination. The dressage horse's mental ability to fulfill his rider's requests develops concurrently with his

muscle strength. You see, a rider's requests sometimes conflict with the horse's natural instincts, which include flight and speed—instincts that are definitely not geared toward collection. However, the real dressage horse ultimately learns to fulfill even the most difficult (and the most beautiful) requirements of the FEI: *"The horse thus gives the impression of doing of his own accord what is required of him. Confident and attentive, he submits generously to the control of his rider"* (**Article 401, Paragraph 3**).

In pink you can see the muscle groups essential to performing collected movements like the piaffe.

temperament

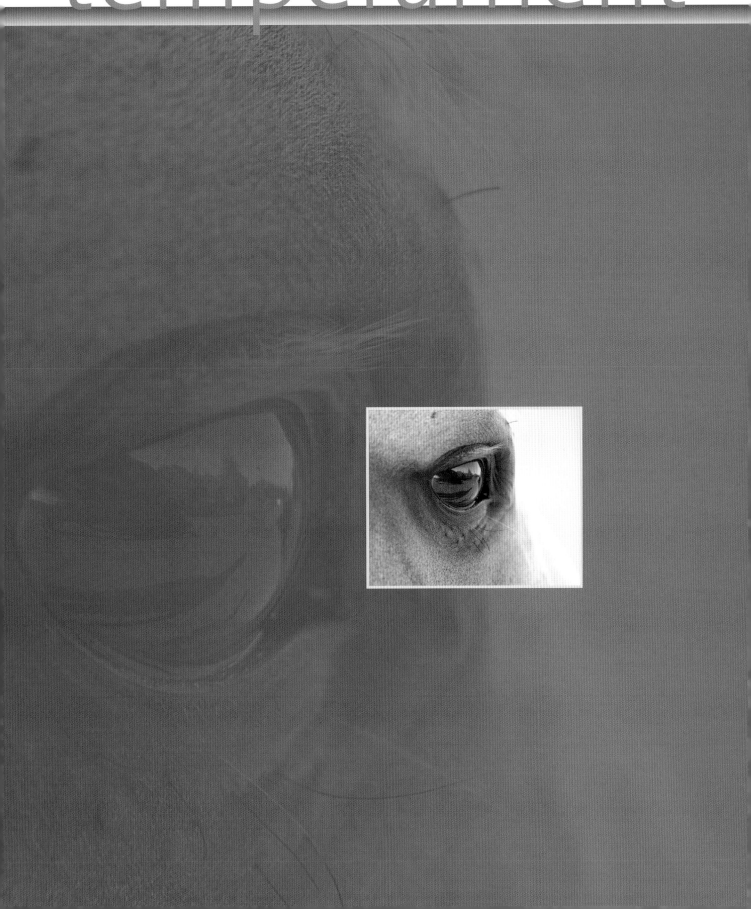

17

The Survey

At the beginning of this book, I stated that we have to take a close look at the temperament of those horses that are successful at the highest levels of dressage. When evaluating a prospect, people tend to focus on what they can see; however, the invisible qualities of a dressage horse are at least as important as, if not more important than, the visible ones.

We began by extensively studying desirable conformation, and then discussed the kind of movement required in a dressage horse, using FEI rules as a guideline for both topics. We arrived at an important conclusion: conformation and movement cannot be viewed one without the other. All the conformational ideals are directly related to the body's use—the horse's movement. For example, the front legs (from hooves to withers) should be long, and the neck should arch upward because when in motion, an "uphill" horse falls on the forehand less than a "downhill" horse. Weak conformation can be directly responsible for poor movement: for example, front legs that stand too far under the body and hind legs that trail behind the body do not facilitate correct and efficient movement.

It was perhaps a mistake to discuss only conformation and movement for sixteen chapters; admittedly, a dressage horse is infinitely more than a collection of bones, tendons, and muscles. And, who other than the rider of a top dressage horse can say which psychological qualities affect the horse-rider relationship and thus the value of a dressage mount? This is why we decided to survey all the upper-level dressage riders in the Netherlands (the ZZGP Foundation riders). The result of this survey is what I hope to be a clear personality sketch of today's top dressage horse.

We thought that the 700 riders who compete at Fourth Level or higher in the Netherlands would be a good source of information, so we sent them all a long list of questions related to their horses' personalities and performance. Despite the amount of time required to answer the questions, 246 of the 700 riders completed and returned the survey—a response rate of 35 percent!

Survey Format

I would like to say a few words about the format of the survey. We borrowed the idea entirely from the doctoral research of Dr. Kathalijne Visser-Riedstra (the Netherlands), who studied the behavior of young jumpers and conducted different tests to measure horse behavior. Her research lead to the dissertation entitled *Horsonality*®, a study of the horse's personality.

Psychologists use five main traits to analyze human behavior (otherwise known as "the Big Five"). They use these concepts, such as willingness, openness to new experiences, and conscientiousness, to describe the major variations in human behavior. Since very little research has been done on the horse's personality, Visser-Riedstra had to similarly establish the main traits of the horse's temperament. She chose three aspects of behavior necessary for a horse, together with a rider, to perform at world-class level: temperament (emotions), social behavior (interaction with people), and the ability to learn.

Visser-Riedstra developed ways to test these three aspects, which together form the horse's "personality."

Horses' temperament was measured by exposing young horses in an indoor arena to an open umbrella that is suddenly dropped (the "new object" test). Social behavior was measured by horse and handler walking together over a "bridge" (a concrete slab laid flat on the ground). Learning ability was measured by whether or not a horse learned to get a reward (grain) and/or learned to avoid an irritating situation (blasts of pressurized air).

Visser-Riedstra's study lead to the assertion, among others, that horse behavior can indeed be quantified (expressed in measurable data) by observing three main traits, using these classifications.

The Survey

Describing the personality of a top dressage horse naturally required us to focus on the behavior of the dressage horse in training and in the arena. The survey sent to our upper-level dressage riders first asked them to describe the temperament, social behavior, and learning ability of their "top" horse—the best horse they ever had. Then, they were asked to describe what they thought the temperament of the ideal dressage horse might be. In addition, respondents were asked to indicate how important they considered each of Visser-Riedstra's three main traits to delivering top performances, and which temperament subtraits and social behaviors have a negative or positive influence on learning ability (for example, opposing traits, such as "lazy/enjoys working" and "dominant/submissive"). Another question concerned the degree to which conformation, movement, and personality had contributed to the success of their best horse. Finally, a separate section examined the individual relationship between each horse and rider.

The Study's Conclusion

Visser-Riedstra's study concluded that of the three main traits, temperament was the most consistent aspect of the horse's personality. This confirms that fearful, enthusiastic, or sensitive horses, for example,

can never really be changed, through training or otherwise. If upper-level riders need to have horses with a specific temperament in order to be successful, then breeders need to know this because these traits are genetic. Naturally, the opposite is just as important: if certain temperament traits are disastrous to a dressage horse's performance, then they must be avoided by breeders.

The goal of our survey was to enable us to fully describe the profile of the top dressage horse. In addition, we wanted to indicate to what extent certain temperament traits contribute to achieving star performances. In the next chapter, we will sketch the personality profile of a top dressage horse, piece by piece.

Dr. Kathalijne Visser-Riedstra laid the foundation for continuing studies of the horse's personality.

18   Opposing Characteristics

A horse is energetic or lazy, brave or timid, sensitive or dull. We suggested in chapter 17 (see p. 90) that little can be done to change a horse's temperament. Regardless how much effort a rider puts into the training process, one cannot change a sluggard into a winning racehorse. So, if the riders who participated in our survey could agree on the emotions vital to a dressage horse, then we could breed for these qualities specifically.

The survey concerning the ideal personality for a top dressage horse began with questions about the horse's emotional behavior because a genetically based "dressage temperament" is extremely important. Our survey is not the first to broach this subject, but the questions we ask are the first to delve into specific areas of emotional behavior. Before we go further, let us digress for a moment and touch upon evolutionary concepts.

The horse's entire body tells us he is a creature of flight: look at his long, light legs, and his natural ability to move across large distances in little time. The horse's psychology also reveals its original function. Horses are relatively nervous animals that are sensitive to changes in their environment, particularly changes that might signal danger. In contrast, the horse's distant cousin, the donkey, has evolved very differently! This territory-bound, defensive animal is the epitome of calm (but far from our athletic ideal).

Explanations of Traits

The horse population includes a wide variety of emo-

tional make-ups. In order to determine the essence of a top dressage horse, we asked riders to describe their best horse using a scale of opposing emotional qualities. An earlier survey of the horse's personality revealed the need to clarify the traits concerned as much as possible. For this reason, we added an extra sentence explaining some of the traits.

The following explanation was added to the opposing traits *lazy* versus *likes to work, enthusiastic, and forward*: "A horse that 'likes to work' moves forward on his own with few driving aids from his rider." *Overly sensitive, quick to resist* as opposed to *persistent, perseverant* was clarified with, "A 'persistent' horse works willingly through pain and fatigue." *Timid* versus *brave* was clarified with, "A 'brave/bold' horse needs little encouragement from his rider in new situations and does not spook as a result of them." *"Looky"* versus *"not looky"* was described as "A 'looky' horse is easily distracted by objects in his environment." *Dull to the aids* as opposed to *very sharp and sensitive* received the following clarification: "A 'sharp, sensitive' horse is very responsive and sensitive to his rider's aids." *Submissive, willing* versus *dominant* was clarified with, "A 'dominant' horse asserts himself strongly against his rider, groom, and others." Finally, *unflappable, even-tempered* versus *sensitive to stress, nervous* was explained with, "A horse that is 'sensitive to stress' and 'nervous' reacts very quickly to changes, sounds, the environment, and other stimuli."

If we were to translate the FEI rules into an outline of the ideal temperament for a dressage horse, it would be as follows: *likes to work, persistent, brave, "not looky," sensitive to the aids, submissive, and unflappable.* Therefore, the opposing qualities include: *lazy, overly*

sensitive, timid, "looky," dull, dominant, and nervous. We created a five-point scale: the ideal quality scored 5 points; negative qualities scored 1 point; and a score of 3 indicated neutrality.

What's Good about a "Workaholic"

According to our survey of riders, their top horse always tended to be very close to ideal in the area of *persistence*. With an average score of 4.30 in this area, we can safely assume that a successful dressage horse continues to work, even when the work becomes more demanding. The same applies to the quality that has a lot to do with effort and the desire to work: *the desire to move*. The average score of 4.14 allows us to assert that horses that reach the top of the sport are enthusiastic and forward. It is remarkable that two traits that taken together can describe "likes to work" score the highest. A top dressage horse is nothing less than a workaholic! Sensitive had an average score of 4.01. In addition, *brave, "not looky,"* and *"submissive"* were also emphasized, although here scores deviated less from

Dressage trainer Conrad Schumacher said Ideaal was a dressage horse with the "ideal" temperament: he enjoyed working and showed natural sensitivity, as well as internal calm. He is pictured here with his rider, Johann Hinnemann.

the neutral score of 3 than with other traits. It would appear that a top dressage horse, on average, is neither overly sensitive to stress nor unflappable.

The Ideal

Not only did we want to sketch the personality profile of those dressage horses actually competing at the top of the sport today, we also asked survey respondents to describe the "ideal temperament." This exercise yielded the same overall data, except that the scores were more extreme, coming closer to the high score of 5. With a score of 4.74, almost everyone is convinced that a good dressage horse must be very *persistent* and he should *like to work* and be *enthusiastic and forward* in order to reach the Grand Prix level (4.52)! *Sharp and sensitive* placed a strong third again, and *"not looky"* scored higher as an ideal quality (3.92) than it had when respondents rated their own dressage horses. We can conclude, therefore, that the *actual* top dressage horse enjoys moving slightly less and is a bit more *"looky"* than the *ideal* top dressage horse.

Let us return for a moment to the evolution of the horse as a flight animal. Which aspects of the ideal temperament are derived from these origins? Certainly the *desire to work, sensitivity,* and—if we use a little imagination—we can even include *persistence* as being somewhat connected to the flight instinct. However, a successful dressage horse must also be *brave* and unflappable, and definitely not *"looky!"* The natural fear and nervousness of the horse, the instincts of a flight animal, stand in the way of the competitive dressage rider reaching his or her goals.

93

The stallion Aktion (Pion x Akteur), bred by B. Ridder in Harkstede, the Netherlands, was an example of the paradox on demand: both hot and cool; and both sensitive and unflappable. Aktion is pictured here ridden by Guylla Dallos.

Conrad Schumacher Weighs In

In 1999, at a symposium with Dr. Hilary Clayton (an expert on the biomechanics of dressage horses—see p. 24), the internationally renowned dressage trainer Conrad Schumacher explained that two-thirds of a top dressage horse's success depends on three main characteristics of his temperament: the desire to work, natural sensitivity, and internal calm. Schumacher used this concept to illustrate the paradox of the ideal dressage temperament: both sensitive *and* unflappable; enthusiastic *and* obedient. Schumacher stated, "In general, horses with a great deal of internal calm are lazy, and very sensitive horses are often crazy and difficult to work with." At that time, Schumacher called Ideaal (Doruto x Eurfraat) a horse that earned his name—he had an ideal temperament for the sport. "Ideaal didn't have great conformation, but he had unbelievable heart!" he explained. "He won his last international medal at age twenty. He really had those three main, very necessary temperament qualities."

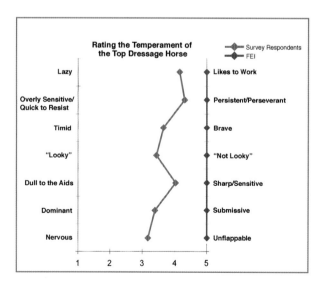

The temperament of survey respondents' top dressage horses and the ideal temperament according to the FEI.

Tenuous Balance

It is a big challenge for breeders to find that tenuous balance between sensitivity and internal calm. Dressage riders ask mainly for qualities associated with the *desire to work* and *sensitivity*, and based on our profile of actual top dressage horses, we gather that the related negative qualities *"looky"* and *nervous* are manageable to riders at this level. However, the continued call for a horse to have more *desire to work* and yet be less *"looky"* reveals how difficult it is to forge two opposite emotions in one temperament.

Horses with perfect, balanced personalities do exist. These horses have proven at Grand Prix level that they can be hot and cool, and sensitive and unflappable on

Table 1 » The *Actual* Top Dressage Horse

Negative Trait	Average	Positive Trait
OVERLY SENSITIVE, QUICK TO RESIST	4.30	PERSISTENT, PERSEVERANT
LAZY	4.14	LIKES TO WORK, ENTHUSIASTIC, FORWARD
DULL TO THE AIDS	4.01	VERY SHARP, SENSITIVE
TIMID	3.65	BRAVE, BOLD
"LOOKY"	3.43	"NOT LOOKY"
DOMINANT	3.38	SUBMISSIVE, WILLING
SENSITIVE TO STRESS, NERVOUS	3.16	UNFLAPPABLE, EASYGOING

NOTE: 1 = EXTREMELY NEGATIVE TRAIT; 3 = NEUTRAL SCORE, 5 = EXTREMELY POSITIVE TRAIT

Table 2 » The *Ideal* Top Dressage Horse

Trait	Average
LIKES TO WORK, ENTHUSIASTIC	4.74
PERSISTENT, PERSEVERANT	4.52
SENSITIVE	4.18
"NOT LOOKY"	3.92
BRAVE, BOLD	3.69

Table 3 » How Important Was/Is the Temperament of Your Top Horse to Your Success Together?

Value	Percentage
EXTREMELY/VERY IMPORTANT	41.2
IMPORTANT	56.3
NOT IMPORTANT/ NOT UNIMPORTANT	1.6
UNIMPORTANT	0.8

demand. Instructor Johan Hamminga remembers the stallion Aktion as a perfect example, "As a young horse, he stood 'sheepishly,' so to speak, behind the grandstands at the stallion selection. However, he hadn't even passed the in-gate when he suddenly 'grew' four inches! You could totally charge him up and then completely bring him back down again, exactly like you wanted."

Aktion, the sire of top dressage horses such as Madeleine Vrees' Feliki, Barbara Koot's Galliano, and Marjan Dorresteijn's Finesse, has been hugely valuable to the dressage breeding industry, for his temperament alone.

19 The Importance of Sociability

The second chapter describing the outcome of our survey deals with social behavior. We asked respondents how their best dressage horse related to people. (We did not, however, ask about the horse's ability to relate to other horses.)

Social behavior between horses is substantially different than social behavior between horses and people. The differences between dominant and submissive horses are evident in horse-person interaction, and the balance of that relationship generally tips in favor of the person. Our mentally superior position allows us to relatively easily take a 1,200-pound, three-year-old that has spent his entire life in a herd of other horses and teach him first to be led by a halter; then to tolerate a girth; and finally to accept a saddle. We can saddle-break a horse, and ultimately he may enjoy doing all sorts of things with a person on his back. It is actually very unique that the horse has evolved into an animal with a survival strategy that allows him to cooperate with humans. It is also unique that the horse accepts his role as the subordinate, with his rider as a sort of "captain at the helm."

Dominant Behavior

It is natural for a horse to recognize people as his superiors, but this says nothing about the horse's relationship with other horses. For example, people cannot prevent horses from determining the "pecking order" of their herd, which is often carried out violently. Punishing a horse for displaying dominant behavior is pointless. If problems arise as a result of this behavior during feeding time, for example, then the best way to deal with it is to physically separate the horses involved. All this suggests that social behavior between horses is a totally different matter than social interaction between horse and rider. The latter relationship, of course, interests us because we want to illustrate the ideal temperament of the successful dressage horse. What exactly happens between horse and rider?

An interactive connection exists when horse and rider work intensely together—a "hotline" of communication. It is not only pleasant but also functionally and competitively significant when the two parties are "on-line" and get along with one another. Imke Schelleken's very emotional response to the sale of Gestion Lancet after the 2004 Olympic games in Athens revealed a great deal: she had not only lost her top international-level horse, but also her friend.

The temperament of people can differ greatly, as well, and they, too, can get along with each other and with different horses very well—or not at all. For these reasons, we next asked our survey participants about the personal bond between rider and horse and the degree to which another rider could have succeeded with this particular horse. Before we discuss this (in chapter 21), I must first explain the questions we posed concerning this issue.

Social Opposites

We asked the respondents to look at three aspects of social behavior, expressed in opposing traits. Respondents had to indicate the extent of a specific behavior using a scale of 1 to 5. The qualities included *sociable, extroverted, friendly* as opposed to *introverted,*

It matters a great deal whether a rider is spending years working with a horse that is a model student or an obstinate beast.

unfriendly, and were clarified with the sentence: "A 'friendly, sociable, extroverted' horse likes people and attention, enjoys being groomed, and eagerly looks out of his stall, watching everything in his environment with interest. In contrast, an 'introverted' horse is content to be alone." *Patient, cooperative, tolerant* were juxtaposed with *dominant*, and the clarifying sentence stated: "A 'dominant' horse defers to his handlers, but requires more than average effort and force." The last set of opposing traits was *easygoing, unflappable* versus *nervous, stress-sensitive*, and was followed by the sentence: "A 'nervous, stress-sensitive' horse reacts quickly to changes in the environment, sound, and the like."

Table 1 (p. 98) shows that our upper-level riders' top horses tend to be *sociable and friendly* rather than *introverted and unfriendly*. The score of 1.80 is not extreme, but clearly leans toward being social. Regarding the degree of *patience* and *tolerance* necessary, the score was 2.26, which is close to the neutral score of 3. *Easygoing and unflappable* also scored close to neutral.

General Assessment

Next, the respondents were asked to indicate how significant they found these traits in general—a 5 meant *very important*, and a 1 *very unimportant*. This part of the survey elicited a more extreme response: riders attached considerable importance to the qualities *sociable, extroverted*, and *patient, cooperative* with scores of 3.90 and 3.92 respectively (Table 2). This suggests that riders really enjoy working with a horse that has a pleasant, cooperative temperament. This is logical if we consider how many hours dressage riders spend training their horses, and how intense communication is between horse and rider.

Sociability Leads to Success

Respondents agree that social behavior is important to achieving success (Table 3). Dressage is obviously more than teaching exercises to a horse that moves well. Top

Table 1 ›› Average Evaluation of the Social Behavior of Survey Respondents' Top Dressage Horse

Positive Trait	Average	Negative Trait
SOCIABLE, EXTROVERTED, FRIENDLY	1.80	INTROVERTED, UNFRIENDLY
PATIENT, COOPERATIVE, TOLERANT	2.26	DOMINANT
EASY-GOING, UNFLAPPABLE	2.63	NERVOUS, STRESS-SENSITIVE

NOTE: 1 = EXTREMELY POSITIVE TRAIT, 3 = NEUTRAL SCORE, 5 = EXTREMELY NEGATIVE TRAIT

Table 2 ›› How Important Are the Following Qualities to a Dressage Horse's Success?

Trait	Average
SOCIABLE, EXTROVERTED, FRIENDLY	3.90
PATIENT, COOPERATIVE, TOLERANT	3.92
EASY-GOING, UNFLAPPABLE	3.78

NOTE: AVERAGE ON A SCALE OF 1 (VERY UNIMPORTANT) TO 5 (VERY IMPORTANT)

Table 3 ›› How Important Was/Is the Social Behavior of Your Top Horse to Your Success Together?

Value	Percentage
EXTREMELY IMPORTANT, VERY IMPORTANT	13.0
IMPORTANT	62.6
NOT IMPORTANT, NOT UNIMPORTANT	23.2
UNIMPORTANT	1.2

Table 4 ›› Average Value for Each Trait by Respondent Age Group

Age	Sociable, Extroverted, Friendly	Patient, Cooperative, Tolerant	Easygoing, Unflappable
14-21	4.08	3.97	3.84
22-30	3.56	3.94	3.50
31-40	3.79	3.77	3.85
▸ 40 +	4.37	4.10	4.00

riders consider competitive dressage a "team sport," in which the partners—rider and horse—share equal responsibility. (We will discuss this more later.) Success is ultimately the product of cooperation and social behavior. Of course, judges do not score the actual social behavior of top dressage horses; however, they do directly score certain aspects of temperament, such as enthusiasm, persistence, and sensitivity.

Sociability contributes to the success of a dressage horse. We can view it as a means to convey a final product: without Styrofoam packaging, an expensive television would not arrive safely at its final destination. A four-year-old, green-broke horse may have incredible conformation, movement, and desire to work; however, getting a horse to the very top of the competitive field will always take many years. Thus, it matters considerably if a rider is working all those years with a horse that is pleasant and willing, or one that is an obstinate beast. We should always ask ourselves if a young eye-catcher with ideal movement and perfect conformation truly has world-class talent if he is continually determined to shut out his rider.

The Impact of Rider Age

When we analyzed the survey, we continually checked to see if significant differences existed between the groups of respondents. For example, do younger riders view certain issues differently than older riders? Young dressage riders (ages 14–21) do value the qualities *sociable, extroverted, friendly* about a half point higher (on a scale of 1 to 5) than the 22–30 age-group. The difference between the latter group and the 40-and-over age-group is even greater. The 40-and-over riders value a pleasant temperament far more than the 22–30 age-group. Finally, the traits *even-tempered, unflappable* yielded very different scores from age-group to age-group (Table 4), suggesting that riders in the "prime" of their lives are more detached from their horse's social behavior than younger and older riders. The older riders surveyed preferred pleasant horses that have predictable temperaments and are easy to work with.

A "sociable" horse is focused on his rider.

20   Learning Ability: A Gray Area

If we look at the differences between a "made" Grand Prix horse and a green three-year-old, we see the differences between a professor and an elementary school student. A Grand Prix horse has not only "read a library of books," he is also one of the few that *understands* these books. Therefore, learning ability is the third important aspect of a dressage horse's personality.

Tests have been developed to rate a person's intelligence quotient (IQ). Perhaps we can do the same for determining a horse's ability to learn dressage exercises. In her dissertation *Horsonality*®, Dr. Kathalijne Visser-Riedstra (an animal behavior scientist from Lelystad, the Netherlands—see p. 90) conducted two experiments that tested horses' learning abilities and revealed a complex picture. In one test, when the participating horses put their noses in their feed bins, they were rewarded with grain falling into a *different* feed bin in the same stall. This same group of horses was also involved in a different experiment that tested their "intellectual" ability to avoid certain situations, in this particular case, having to endure blasts of pressurized air.

While both tests individually revealed "smart" and "dumb" horses, the results proved complicated, for no truly clear pattern emerged when the tests were considered together. The "smart" horses that quickly figured out how to get a food reward (in the feed-bin test) were not the same horses that were intelligent enough to figure out how to avoid an unpleasant experience in the second test.

The learning ability of the horse is difficult to measure. However, we certainly know that it exists: every rider knows the difference between horses that learn quickly—and seem eager to learn—and horses that are slow to learn and seem to have little interest in the process.

The previous chapter discussed how the opposing temperament traits *submissiveness* and *dominance* impact the degree to which a horse is open to communicating with his rider. A submissive horse that readily agrees to comply with his rider's aids not only communicates better with his rider, he will learn new exercises faster because of it. Although we divided our discussion of scientific research on horse behavior into three chapters, there are, of course, areas where personality traits overlap.

The Positive

The rider survey we constructed was not intended to completely describe the various aspects of equine learning ability. We mainly wanted to know the sort of qualities required for a dressage horse to be able to successfully "read through and understand a library of academic books." For this reason, we asked respondents which temperament qualities have a positive correlation with enhanced learning ability. Along with the new qualities *perceptive, intelligent,* we selected several traits discussed in earlier chapters.

It is remarkable that *enthusiastic, likes to work* were named the most valuable traits (72 percent), in that they were clearly more desirable than *perceptive, intelligent*—the obvious traits in this context (64.6 percent). *Persistent, perseverant* scored high, as well (61.8 percent). These survey results once again prove that everything depends on the horse's *desire to work*. The desire to remain as physically active when in extreme collection as when performing a normal working gait is necessary to actually perform the piaffe and pirouette, but also—even more so—to first learn these difficult exercises. In addition, *patient, cooperative, tolerant* and *sensitive* were quite often cited as traits that support learning ability.

The Negative

Naturally, we posed the opposite question: Which qualities negatively affect learning ability? In fact, negative aspects of temperament and social behavior were named far less often than those that affect the horse's learning ability positively. We can actually only name two qualities that clearly appear to have a negative effect. *Stress-sensitive, nervous* and *"looky"* were cited more than half the time as learning obstacles (Table 2). *Sensitive* was also labeled a negative quality at times (17.5 percent), as the area between *sensitive* and *nervous* is unfortunately rather gray. What's more, a sensitive horse can learn a great deal with one rider and nothing at all with another.

Pressure and Release

A horse's ability to learn is only truly revealed when he begins his training. What happens when the horse and rider communicate? If all goes well and the horse displays the desired behavior, he receives a reward, such as a pat on the neck or a "good boy!" (positive reinforcement). On the other hand, a rider might punish the horse for undesired behavior with a flick of the whip (negative reinforcement). However, a rider can use a third technique, one that is often implemented but is actually the least recognized of the three: pressure and release. We often use this by applying pressure and then releasing the pressure when the horse reacts appropriately. For example, pressure on the mouth results in flexion, and that pressure diminishes when the rider gets the desired result. A rider teaches a horse to move laterally by putting leg pressure on the horse's side, and the rider removes the pressure if the horse responds appropriately to the aid. Therefore, we have three ways to affect positive learning: reward, punishment, and pressure and release.

We asked our survey riders which of these techniques they used and to what degree. We also looked at the differences between the rider's age-groups on this topic (Table 3).

Table 1 » Traits Most Often Named to *Positively* Affect the Horse's Learning Ability

Trait	Percentage
ENTHUSIASTIC, LIKES TO WORK	72.0
PERCEPTIVE, INTELLIGENT	64.6
PERSISTENT, PERSEVERANT	61.8
PATIENT, COOPERATIVE, TOLERANT	59.3
SENSITIVE	50.8

Table 2 » Traits Most Often Named to *Negatively* Affect the Horse's Learning Ability

Trait	Percentage
STRESS-SENSITIVE, NERVOUS	59.8
"LOOKY"	55.3
DOMINANT	26.0
SENSITIVE	17.5

Table 3 » Types of Teaching Methods Used with Top Dressage Horses (Percent by Rider Age-Group)

	14-21	22-30	31-40	> 40
REWARD ALMOST EXCLUSIVELY	8.6	8.7	14.5	14.6
PRESSURE AND RELEASE ALMOST EXCLUSIVELY	0.0	5.8	0.0	6.3
PUNISH ALMOST EXCLUSIVELY	0.0	0.0	0.0	0.0
MAINLY REWARD/PRESSURE AND RELEASE	57.1	65.2	73.5	64.6
MAINLY PUNISH	0.0	0.0	0.0	0.0
REWARD, PRESSURE AND RELEASE AND PUNISH EQUALLY	34.3	20.3	12.0	14.6

Table 4 » When Do You Use Punishment during Training?

	Percentage
RESISTANCE (BUCKING, REARING, STOPPING)	25.6
NOT RESPONDING TO AIDS, LITTLE EFFORT	72.4
SPOOKING FOR NO REASON	4.1
NEVER OR SELDOM PUNISH	6.5
OTHER (GROUND MANNERS, ETC.)	2.0

Table 5 » Was/Is Your Best Horse's Learning Ability Greater than That of Your Other Horses?

	Percentage
YES	57.8
NO	15.6
JUST AS GREAT	15.2
DON'T KNOW	11.5

Table 6 » How Important Was/Is Your Best Horse's Learning Ability to Your Competitive Success with Him?

	Percentage
EXTREMELY IMPORTANT, VERY IMPORTANT	35.1
IMPORTANT	60.0
NOT IMPORTANT, NOT UNIMPORTANT	4.5
UNIMPORTANT	0.4
NOTE: AVERAGED ON A SCALE OF 1 (VERY UNIMPORTANT) TO 5 (VERY IMPORTANT)	

Training Method by Age-Group

The vast majority of respondents in all age groups indicated that they achieve positive training results through a combination of reward- and pressure-and-release-based learning. The youngest respondents use pressure and release the least. Those who use equal amounts of reward, pressure and release, and punishment are ages 14–21, the largest group. Older riders, those 31–40 and 40-and-over, use punishment far less often than the younger groups. No one named punishment as their sole method of training. Older riders constitute the significant majority of those who *only* use reward-based training. The older the rider, the less value that rider sees in using punishment as a positive teaching method and the more inclined that rider is to reward his or her horse. When do dressage riders punish their horses? The vast majority said they punish their horses only when their horses respond insufficiently to their aids (Table 4).

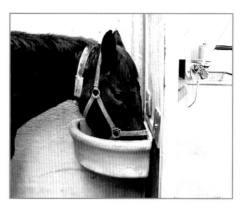

Dr. Kathalijne Visser-Riedstra conducted two experiments to test horses' learning abilities. Those that excelled in the test where they were rewarded for a reaction were not the same horses that did well in the test where they had to avoid discomfort. Visser-Riedstra's research dealt with factors that determine the quality of a jumper.

No Difference in Learning Ability

Surprisingly, many dressage riders (more than 30 percent of those surveyed) do not think that the learning ability of their top horse is any greater than that of their other horses (Table 5). Do horses fare better than we might expect with that "library of academic books," or is the horse's IQ such complicated territory that we cannot understand it? Or, do some riders simply think, "Just give me a horse that likes to work and isn't too obstinate, and I'll teach him those movements no matter what!"

Learning Ability and Success

Just as with the sections on equine temperament and social behavior, our last question concerns how important learning ability is to a horse's success. The previous chapters revealed that riders considered a horse's social behavior important, but not as important as his temperament. Dressage riders are well aware that they cannot change a horse's personality, and those qualities, such as the *desire to work* and *perseverance*, must be inherent.

As we expected, riders also considered learning ability to be more important than social behavior; however, more riders felt that temperament was extremely important than those who felt the same about learning ability (Table 6).

21 The Horse and Rider Partnership

Dressage is a team sport. This "team" consists of two individuals who are intensely focused on one another, each of whom makes an essential contribution. The last question on our survey pertained to the all-important relationship between horse and rider.

There are few Anky van Grunsvens in the world—riders who manage to remain on top with apparent ease while their first Grand Prix horse enjoys his retirement in the pasture. Usually, a good rider is dependant on that infamous once-in-a-lifetime, world-class horse: Nicole Uphoff needed Rembrandt to win medals; Anne-Grethe Jensen could not seem to win international competitions after Marzog; and Margit Otto-Crépin never again achieved top rankings after Corlandus.

Anky van Grunsven confirms that at the pinnacle of international competitive dressage, a horse's unique talent determines whether or not one wins medals. Of course, even the very best horse needs a very good rider to reach Grand Prix; however, once the rider has attained that level, then the horse's ability is what makes the difference.

The Genetic "Glass Ceiling"

Every horse has a genetic "glass ceiling." After years of training, each horse eventually reaches the end of his athletic capabilities and taps out his drive to perform. Even the best rider and trainer in the world working together cannot remove that ceiling. Alongside the horse's ability, the rider needs a tremendous amount of skill to train a horse to his full potential and to show him at his best in front of a panel of judges and an audience.

The division of the roles within the dressage "team" is an interesting subject of study. The survey revealed more information regarding the extent to which riders and top dressage horses contribute to their combined success. A significant majority (63.7 percent) thought that rider and horse contributed equally. The largest minority (21.2 percent) believed that success was 75 percent due to the horse and 25 percent to the rider. Only 12.7 percent felt that the rider contributed the greatest share (Table 1). Age did not seem to impact these feelings, as both younger and older riders agreed that the team's success was due to an equal contribution.

Next, we asked our participating riders if they thought that another rider with comparable riding ability would have had as much success with their top horse as they had experienced. A correlation analysis involving the previous question ("What share did the rider have and what share did the horse have in the team's success?") revealed that those respondents who answered, "As the rider, I was responsible for 75 percent of our success," more often responded, "No, a comparable rider would not have achieved as much success with my top horse as I did" (Table 2). This small group of riders either believes in special partnerships between riders and horses, or they are very convinced of their own riding ability!

Why Would a Different Rider Have Less Success?

The answer to the question is more important than the question itself. Approximately half the riders surveyed

Table 1 » What Share Did the Rider Have and What Share Did the Horse Have in the Team's Success?

	Percentage
MY TOP HORSE CONTRIBUTED THE GREATEST SHARE	2.4
MY TOP HORSE CONTRIBUTED A SIGNIFICANT SHARE	21.2
MY TOP HORSE AND I CONTRIBUTED EQUALLY	63.7
I CONTRIBUTED A SIGNIFICANT SHARE	12.7
I CONTRIBUTED THE GREATEST SHARE	0.0

Table 2 » Would a Comparable Rider Have As Much or Less Success with Your Best Horse (Percent Based on the Share Rider and Horse Had in Team's Success)?

	Horse (>75%)	Horse (>50%)	Equal	Rider (>50%)	Rider (>75%)	Average
LESS SUCCESS	20.0%	48.8	55.2	74.1	0	49.5
AS MUCH SUCCESS	80.0	51.2	44.8	25.9	0	50.4

Table 3 » Which Characteristics Would Contribute to a Rider with Comparable Riding Ability Having *Less* Success with Your Best Horse?

Trait	Percentage
SENSITIVE	32.5
STRESS-SENSITIVE, NERVOUS	24.0
"LOOKY"	20.7
DOMINANT	11.4

Table 4 » Which Characteristics Would Contribute to a Rider with Comparable Riding Ability Having As *Much* Success with Your Best Horse?

Trait	Percentage
ENTHUSIASTIC, LIKES TO WORK	21.5
PATIENT, COOPERATIVE, TOLERANT	19.9
PERCEPTIVE, INTELLIGENT	19.5
PERSISTENT, PERSEVERANT	11.8
SENSITIVE	8.9

think that a different good rider would have had less success with the same horse, which is a slight advantage for proponents of the idea that a special relationship can exist between a rider and horse. We asked the following question: "Why would another good rider have had less success with your top horse?" and allowed the respondents to select from the series of traits that were also used in our previous discussions regarding equine temperament, social behavior, and learning ability (Table 3). *Sensitive* ranks number one on the table, which is logical given that we are discussing top dressage horses. Our profile of the dressage horse's ideal temperament places *sensitivity* third, for it contributes to the horse's ability to reach the upper levels of competition. However, it can also be a *negative* quality, as illustrated in the chapter on learning ability (see p. 000). When riders were asked to indicate which temperament traits affected a horse's learning ability positively or negatively, they named *sensitivity* as both a positive as well as a negative influence. A sensitive horse demands more from his rider; the rider must be more patient and take the horse's idiosyncrasies into account, which may lead a rider to think they share a special relationship.

The other traits that led respondents to think that a comparable rider would have less success with his or her top horse were the same four traits that they felt have a negative influence on a horse's learning ability.

Why Would a Different Rider Have As Much Success?

We naturally presented the same question to survey participants who thought that another rider could have just as much success with their top horse as they had. We asked them the traits responsible for this (Table 4), and they answered very similarly to earlier answers regarding characteristics that have a positive effect on equine learning ability: an *enthusiastic, patient, intelligent,* and *persistent* horse is easy to ride and could potentially win with any other rider of comparable ability.

A fine example of this is Bo (registered name Berna; Rinaldo x Komeet), bred by W. van der Noll in 's-Gravezande, the Netherlands. This mare, born in 1983, won the European team bronze with Sjef Janssen and subsequently was successful with Sven and Gonnelien Rothenberger. Jo Rutten took Ampére (J. Amagun x Important), bred by P. Stassen in Venlo, the Netherlands, to the top, after which Gina Capellmann became his rider, also winning medals. A previous chapter mentioned Ideaal (Doruto x Eufraat), bred by P.L. Aarts in Heeswijk-Dinther, the Netherlands, as an example of a horse with a wonderful temperament. Johann Hinnemann achieved international success with this Doruto son, and then later on, Sven and Gonnelien Rothenberger succeeded with him, as well.

Table 5 » How Much Does a Horse's Conformation, Movement, and Temperament Contribute to His Performance?

	Percentage
CONFORMATION	26.22
MOVEMENT	37.39
TEMPERAMENT	36.32

Just like all top dressage riders, Nicole Uphoff needed a great partner—the world-class Rembrandt—to win medals.

Jo Rutten took Ampére (J. Amagun x Important) to the Grand Prix level. Then Gina Capellmann became Ampére's rider and won medals in 1986 and 1987.

An "Uncomplicated" Temperament

44.5 percent of the riders who said that another rider could have achieved just as much success with their top horse as they had thought their horses were rather uncomplicated, while the other 55.5 percent considered their best horses to be more "delicate" on average.

This information reminds us of what Conrad Schumacher touched upon when he spoke about the ideal (although not easy to find) combination of natural sensitivity and inner calm in a horse. In any case, this survey also shows how important it is for breeders to strive for horses that are nice to ride and have uncomplicated temperaments. Of course, a studbook must provide talented horses, but it is also important that a number of good riders can test and develop these talents.

Weighing Three Factors

So, what is the composition of a top dressage horse? I have suggested that the success of a dressage horse is dependent on three factors: conformation, movement, and temperament. We asked the riders in our survey what share these three factors had in the their best horse's success, and they indicated that movement and temperament played equal roles in their success, but they felt a top dressage horse's conformation also contributed substantially (Table 5).

Confirming the Importance of Temperament

We asked the same question with respect to the three main traits of the horse's temperament: *temperament, social behavior,* and *learning ability* (Table 6). The dressage horse's "emotions" and intelligence carried the most weight in terms of performance; however, we should not ignore the horse's social behavior and how his tendencies impact his relationship with his rider.

Kyra and Matador

Striking examples of horse-and-rider pairs devoted to one another include Rembrandt and Nicole Uphoff, and Matador and Kyra Kyrklund. Both horses were at the top of their game when they were confronted with serious physical problems (a broken leg and colic surgery, respectively), and yet ultimately returned successfully due, in part, to the intense bond they shared with their riders.

Kyra Kyrklund describes Matador—the best horse she's had in her life—as "very energetic, enthusiastic, and a little unsure." This is entirely consistent with the temperament of the "average top" dressage horse, as indicated by our survey. In addition, Kyra immediately recognizes perseverance as *essential* for a top dressage horse. "Just like with people, there are big differences between horses when it comes to sensitivity to pain and fatigue," she says. "The ones that say in the morning, 'Oh, I have a headache; I'm not going to work' are the ones you really don't want for competitive dressage. Matador was a bit insecure and sensitive to noises his entire life, although he didn't really spook at things. If he looked at something, then that was more an excuse to blow off some of his tremendous energy. However, he could work through fatigue without question."

Kyra noticed a change in Matador's personality after his difficult colic surgery. "He had more self-confidence; he wasn't as insecure. I think that's because he constantly had people around him who gave him a lot of attention, and not just me." At first, Matador did not do well after the surgery. Kyra says, "I rode him, but he wasn't the same horse anymore. I got the feeling he wasn't just physically affected by having major surgery; he was also suffering from serious mental depression. Then, one day, a group of school children on a field trip came to the barn, so we braided Matador beautifully, and dressed him up as though we were going to a show. When Matador entered the arena, we saw him change: he was the performer again; he had the attention of an audience, and he was doing what he enjoyed doing the most. And, that's how Matador got a new start.

Table 6 » How Much Do the Personality Traits Temperament, Social Behavior, and Learning Ability Contribute to a Top Dressage Horse's Performance?

	Percentage
Temperament	37.74
Social Behavior	24.56
Learning Ability	37.63

Bo (Rinaldo x Comet), ridden by Sjef Janssen, was successful at the 1991 European Championship. He then went on to international dressage success with Sven Rothenberger and Gonnelien Rothenberger-Gordijn.

Kyra Kyrklund said the following about Matador (Sire: May Sheriv): "Matador totally fit the image of a persistent horse that likes to work. Our bond changed after his colic surgery, and every day became a day to enjoy."

"My relationship with Matador changed after his surgery. Before the surgery, I was more uptight and tended to react negatively when things didn't go that well or when we weren't having a very good day. After the surgery, I realized just how fortunate I was to have this special horse to ride. Every day was a day to enjoy. I became more relaxed; the pressure was gone. As a result, success came to us again, and relatively easy."

109

22 "When I Drop the Reins, the World Opens Up Again"

As history has proven, Anky van Grunsven's personality jibes with "highly explosive" horses. Could any other rider have won the gold in Sydney and Athens on Bonfire and Salinero?

When you ask Anky about the temperament of her horses, she reveals the complicated mix comprised of sensitivity, enthusiasm, "lookiness," and learning ability. "A sensitive horse is quick and responsive, which is really nice for a rider," says Anky. "However, this kind of horse will also react suddenly to a bouquet of flowers or a photographer, and this problem is something a rider needs to learn to solve with confidence."

Just like the ZZGP Foundation riders, Anky van Grunsven completed our survey regarding the personality of top dressage horses. She completed the survey individually for each of her three top horses: Bonfire, Salinero, and Krack C.

"I found it difficult to say whether someone else could have had as much success with my top horse," reflects Anky. "I don't let others try my horses! Of course, it's indeed true that certain horses will never achieve their full potential with some riders. I think I have a few horses in my barn that wouldn't really be a good match with anyone else, and I have students' horses that wouldn't really be good matches for me. There are some horses that need little physical effort from their riders to perform—I think these are the best horses because they present a nice picture sooner than horses that require a lot of work. There are good riders who can't get along with real sensitive horses, but I'll take one any day!"

General Views on Temperament

"A very sensitive horse is more likely to be *afraid* and *'looky'* than a less sensitive one. These horses react to many stimuli and react to them very quickly. Thus, they respond easily to light aids, but of course, they respond to things they shouldn't, too! This is why I scored Bonfire more toward afraid and 'looky' on the survey, although he was much worse when we started out together. When Bonfire was young, he was very nervous; later, he became a lot more easygoing. It's exactly the same now with Salinero. A 'super-alert' horse keeps getting easier to manage," says Anky.

Our survey included a space where riders could express their general views on the temperament necessary for a dressage horse to be successful. A "5" indicated that respondents considered a trait essential; a "1" indicated a trait was very unimportant. Anky revealed, "I put down the maximum '5' for *likes to work*, *enthusiastic* as well as for *persistent*, *perseverant*, and *sensitive*. I gave *brave* and *bold* a '3' because I don't think they're very important. And dominant doesn't matter to me at all. I gave *stress-sensitive* a '2.' I don't consider it a problem if a good horse is nervous because I think that goes away on its own. A 'looky' horse will always be 'looky,' even when he's twenty-one years old. However, if that horse trusts you, and you trust him, then there's less stress."

Special Approach

"Horses like Bonfire and Salinero definitely require a special approach. Everything is easy for them, so they're inclined to be distracted and focus on other

"With Bonfire especially, I had to stay busy constantly. I still remember what Sjef said every time we went in the ring: 'Think of something to keep him with you.'"

things. If you give them the chance, they'll come up with some reason to be distracted on their own. You can't just sit nice-and-quiet and think everything will be fine. With Bonfire especially, I had to stay constantly busy. I still remember what Sjef said every time we went in the ring: 'Keep him busy; think of something to keep him with you.' It could be a momentary transition or a small play of the rein that no one sees. The horse has to think, 'What exactly does she want from me now?' You need that to keep him focused on you. That's what it's about: he's focusing on you and not on the bouquet of flowers or the television camera.

"We're super focused during a test as well as in training—me on my horse and my horse on me. It's as though the world closes in around us. We only pay attention to one another. I don't understand riders who say that they saw 'this' or 'that' happen during a test. I never see anything until the test is over. When I drop the reins, the world opens up again. What happened with Bonfire in Sydney was very typical: everything was fine in the arena, but outside, I had trouble getting him passed *anything* by myself. My horses learn that nothing happens to them in the arena; they can count on that," says Anky.

The Same Fire

Bonfire and Salinero are very similar with respect to their temperaments. The same fire burns in both horses. However, Anky built the bond of trust with Salinero much faster than with Bonfire. In Athens, we saw Salinero change over the course of a couple of days from a frightened animal to a relaxed, elite athlete, completely focused on his rider.

"Accomplishing that change was largely a matter of experience," notes Anky. "I can now feel how I should react to a certain situation much faster than I once did—but there were other factors in Athens. The stadium was very messy the first day, but it was cleaned up later."

When asked how important specific personality aspects were to her success with her top horses, Anky responded the same for all three horses: a horse's temperament and learning ability were *extremely important*; and social behavior was *not important/not unimportant*. Anky says, "I personally think it's important that a horse is sociable and friendly, but those qualities don't help me ride or perform better.

"Bonfire is sometimes cranky in his stall, or he stands

in a corner. However, when I ride him, we're totally on the same page. Cocktail was my teddy bear; I was crazy about that horse. However, I couldn't count on him nearly as much, of course, partly because he was a stallion, which made him much less consistent mentally," reveals Anky.

According to Anky, horses' learning abilities vary considerably: "After only a week of training, I can recognize the horses that are quick to remember and pick things up. You don't have to be riding Grand Prix to figure this out. You can't predict how far a five-year-old will go. I think it all works together: the sensitivity, nervousness, 'lookiness,' but also that ability to learn—being open to signals from the environment as well as the rider. A sensitive horse is quick to spook at a bunch of flowers but is also quick to learn exercises. I've sold horses in the past because they lacked learning ability, but they also lacked sensitivity. It was a combination of factors."

One Step Ahead

Anky says, "It can also work against you if a horse is smarter than you—or quicker, in any case! Right now,

Salinero is my most difficult horse because he's my most intelligent. He's often one step ahead of me. If I've practiced something twice with him, then he takes the initiative the third time—but I want to be the one who decides what happens. Fortunately, he doesn't resist me, but I have to pay ten times more attention in communicating with Salinero than with other horses."

Bonfire's and Salinero's temperaments share important similarities: they are quick, intelligent, sensitive, and "looky" horses. "My best Grand Prix horses weren't that successful on the small tour," reflects Anky. "In the beginning, they were too hot and nervous. The nervous part of this temperament takes a lot of time, but what's left over in the end—the sensitivity, the drive, the expression—that's definitely what it's all about at the Grand Prix level."

Krack C is a bit different, although not with respect to his *desire to work* and *perseverance* (for which Anky gave him the maximum score). She says, "He is braver—not as 'looky'—as Bonfire and Salinero. Krack is certainly sensitive enough for me but not extremely sensitive like Bonnie and Sallie. Another rider may have scored Krack the maximum for sensitivity. I score

"*Krack is much different, socially speaking than Bonfire: he's very friendly, very patient, and fairly unflappable.*"

"*Salinero is my most difficult horse because he is my most intelligent.*"

ANKY VAN GRUNSVEN

What is *Punishment?*

I consider *overly-sensitive* and *quick to resist* very different things, just like I do *introverted* and *unfriendly*, and age can really be a determining factor for some traits like *stress-sensitive, nervous,* and *"looky."* Sometimes a young horse is very nervous but gets better with age.

I thought the section on pressure-and-release-based training was difficult, although I have an idea of what it's about. I feel giving a horse an aid to which he is trained to respond is different than if he learns to *avoid an unpleasant situation.* It's quite difficult to talk about these things. For example, how do you define *punishment?* One person will smack her horse ten times with a whip and call that punishment, while another considers a small poke of the spurs punishment enough. I use my voice a lot, and if one aid is not effective, then I give a clearer aid. In my mind, that's also punishment.

him more toward *stress-sensitive* because he certainly is, but he doesn't show it that much. Krack is much different in his social behavior than Bonfire: he's very friendly, very patient, and fairly unflappable. Salinero is also very sociable in his stall, but on the ground, he's a bit dominant and sensitive to stress."

A Team Effort

When the survey asked the degree to which her success could be attributed to her riding or her horse's abilities, Anky responded, "I answered in the middle with all three horses. Regardless of the horse and the level you ride, it's always a team effort."

In regard to the importance of conformation, movement, and temperament to the success of dressage horses, she says, "I put down 10 percent for conformation for all three of my horses; I think move-

ment and temperament are much more important. Of course, I also know that if a horse has bad conformation, he can't move. I didn't score my horses' social behavior high in any of the cases. If I only rode for fun, then that percentage would naturally be much higher. However, for competitive dressage, it matters very little if a horse is sociable. Bonnie isn't sociable at all; he couldn't care less. He always says, 'Leave me alone.' Temperament and learning ability are indeed very important. It happens between the ears. The *desire to work* must be inherent."

The survey also asked whether riders preferred a certain sex for their dressage horses. "I prefer to ride geldings," admits Anky. "However, I'm glad Krack is a stallion; otherwise, I wouldn't have had the opportunity to ride him. Sometimes it's just that simple. Stallions are more difficult, though, just because of breeding season alone."

The Happy Athlete

At the time this book was written, the FEI announced a change in the formulation of its most important dressage article: **Chapter 1, Article 401, Paragraph 1** articulates the goal of competitive dressage. This article previously referenced the development of the organism and the natural qualities of the horse, but after much discussion regarding the ambiguity of this wording, the term "happy athlete" was launched as the concise characterization of the essence of competitive dressage. The article now states: *"The object of dressage is the development of the horse into a happy athlete through harmonious education."*

The goal of this book is to provide a blueprint for the ideal dressage horse, one that performs his work inside the dressage arena easily and gladly. For these reasons, I'll discuss the term "happy athlete" in this epilogue.

Remarkable Standard

At first glance, the term "happy athlete" is a remarkable standard. After all, a horse that performs a dressage test is not visibly happy or unhappy. He does not find enjoyment in an awards ceremony, and he does not succumb to a bad mood if he sees the judge who gave him low scores at a show the previous week. A horse's mental well-being is primarily linked to his physical self, and actually this physical method of experiencing of well-being makes "happy athlete" a very appropriate term! After all, a dressage horse is an athlete; his work is both physically and mentally difficult. A horse with a great deal of talent will likely enjoy this work more than one with little talent who must constantly struggle. Likewise, a well-ridden horse will be "happier" than one whose rider is not very skilled. And, compare a horse that is shown below the level to which he is trained to a horse that is still too young or inexperienced for the level at which he is being competed.

Many factors that concern this so-called "harmonious development" of the horse can be expressed in terms of happiness or well-being. A horse that is ridden with a very short neck does not carry his neck that way because he enjoys doing so, and in that respect, may be less "happy" than a horse that moves with a nice, steady contact but with his head slightly in front of the vertical. Of course, these factors comprise part of the existing arsenal of evaluation criteria. Judges and trainers should consider the "happy athlete rule" an extra instrument to safeguard the ultimate goal of dressage.

Signs of Well-Being

How can we assess something as intangible as well-being? We can see the differences between horses that are forward, cooperative, relaxed, and on-the-bit to varying degrees—but what *exactly* are the signs of well-being that can be evaluated in this context?

The position and movement of the ears can reveal a horse that is resistant due to pain or extreme fatigue. The eyes can express nervousness or other negative emotions. Tension in the topline can indicate psychological tension; lack of lateral bend can indicate that a horse finds a particular exercise very difficult. An open mouth may be proof that a horse is high-strung and does not have that ideal "line of communication" with his rider. In many cases, a swishing tail is a sign of unease or protest.

However, a horse may just be a little stiff through his body; he may swish his tail "meaninglessly;" or habitually flap a lip. If tail swishing and lip flapping begin to be considered sure signs of "unhappiness," then I fear they will take on an unintended life of their own.

The Total Picture

Just like everything judges evaluate, these assessments must be considered in light of the whole picture. A horse that is completely relaxed and regular in his movement in piaffe—and flaps his mouth—should, of course, be evaluated completely differently from one that does something similar with his mouth in the same exercise but is held tightly in place with the curb rein.

The term "happy athlete" does not revolutionize the way competitive dressage is evaluated. It does, however, encourage judges to place horses on top that respond to the difficult demands of dressage with physical ease and apparent enjoyment. In addition, it is a weapon judges can use to protect horses from riders who mistakenly think a dressage horse is a possession to be used at their disposal.

ANKY
VAN GRUNSVEN

A Good Resource

I think the "happy athlete" is a good resource for judging dressage tests. Dressage has to be fun for both rider and horse. It also has to be fun for judges and audiences to watch.

Competitive Grand Prix dressage consists almost exclusively of "happy athletes": horses that do what they're good at and what they like to do. As Grand Prix level dressage riders, we also need to set a good example. It wouldn't be good if we didn't have a bit of an edge over dressage as a whole. For this reason, I think it's very important that the principle "happy athlete" also extend to the levels below Grand Prix. There's indeed work to be done, although a good start has been made. For example, enter at "A" and halt at "X" has been repealed for the lowest levels in the Netherlands, which I think is very good because the way a horse moves and the way a specific movement is performed is more important for young horses and inexperienced riders than doing movements precisely at the letters.

A resistant horse that basically "survives" a test has little to do with dressage and absolutely nothing to do with a *happy athlete*!

Acknowledgments

Many more people contributed to this book than just those mentioned on the dust jacket. The first person I want to thank is P. René van Weeren, DVM, and Associate Professor on the faculty of Veterinary Medicine at Utrecht University, the Netherlands. René is one of the most knowledgeable and intelligent people I know. In the midst of night duty, colic operations, and international meetings, he always found time to save me from veterinary and biomechanical blunders. René opened a world for me that will ideally be opened for many more people. Those who are committed to a sport with an animal as a partner do not have to be labeled as crazy (although we are crazy if we do not deepen our knowledge of what evolution has handed down to us!) Thanks to people like René van Weeren, we have a better idea of what horses experience in life and athletics.

Anky van Grunsven broke her leg "at exactly the right time" and so for a short while had more time than usual to put her brilliant feel for horses into words. Off-the-cuff, critical, and lighthearted: she performed her job beautifully, providing a counterbalance to theory. My admiration for this talented rider increased; I respect her not only for her ability in the saddle, but also as a woman who really thinks about her profession.

The work of Dr. Kathalijne Visser-Riedstra laid a solid foundation for research on horse behavior—it served as a foundation upon which to build our survey. Furthermore, Kathalijne generously contributed to the content of the questions we posed to the ZZGP Foundation riders.

Artist Mary-Ellen Janssen allowed us to see the moving horse in an amazing way with her watercolors.

Because of my involvement with the KWPN, I am very privileged to be able to meet the best riders, trainers, scientists, and horses in the world.

Many thanks also to Thieu van Gansewinkel, the secretary of the ZZGP Foundation, who helped established our connection with dressage riders in the Netherlands. He did a great job: 35 percent of his members felt sufficiently compelled to answer the survey. Thank you very much.

Claartje van Andel spent a great deal of her time compiling and processing the survey. Two communications studies students did the actual analysis: Wieteke Jongbloed and Anne-Lotte Paymans. The quality of their report is impressive.

Frenk Jespers was kind enough to give his expert commentary on the chapters dealing with the basic gaits. Discussions with my wife, Anne Rosie-Boogman and her friend, Marjon Hoen, also lead to subsequent improvements or refinements.

Thank you very much everyone!

Dirk Willem Rosie

References

» Back, Willem and Hilary M. Clayton, eds. 2002. *Equine Locomotion*. Philadelphia: W.B. Saunders Company. [ISBN 0-7020-2483-X. An English language collection of 16 scientific essays.]

» Back, Willem. 2002. Intra-limb coordination: the fore limb and the hind limb. In *Equine Locomotion* edited by Willem Back and Hilary M. Clayton. Philadelphia: W.B. Saunders Company. [ISBN 0-7020-2483-X]

» Barrey, Eric. 2002. Intra-limb coordination. In *Equine Locomotion* edited by Willem Back and Hilary M. Clayton. Philadelphia: W.B. Saunders Company. [ISBN 0-7020-2483-X]

» Budiansky, Stephen. 1997. *The Nature of Horses: Exploring Equine Evolution, Intelligence and Behavior*. New York: The Free Press. [ISBN 90-274-7680-2. A popular science book that describes the history, evolution, and nature of the horse across the full scope of its function.]

» Clayton, Hilary M. 2002. Performance in equestrian sports. In *Equine Locomotion* edited by Willem Back and Hilary M. Clayton. Philadelphia: W.B. Saunders Company. [ISBN 0-7020-2483-X.]

» De Groot, D., Ducro, B.J., Koenen, E.P.L. and J.M.F.M. van Tartwijk. 2002. Genetic correlations between conformation traits of Dutch warmblood horses and performance in competition: show jumping and dressage. Ph.D. diss., Wageningen University, the Netherlands.

» Fédération Equestre Internationale (FEI). 2003. Règlement des concours de dressage [rules for dressage events]. *FEI Rulebook*. Lausanne, Switzerland.

» Holmström, Mikael. 2002. The effects of conformation. In *Equine Locomotion* edited by Willem Back and Hilary M. Clayton. Philadelphia: W.B. Saunders Company. [ISBN 0-7020-2483-X]

» Huizinga, H.A., van der Werf, J.H.J., Korver, S. and G.J.W. van der Meij. 1991. stationary performance testing of stallions form the Dutch warmblood riding horse population. 1. estimated genetic parameters of scored traits and the genetic relation with dressage and jumping competition from offspring of breeding stallions. *Livest. Prod. Sci.* 27, 231-244.

» Thorén, E., Gelinder, A., Bruns, E. and J. Philipsson. 2002. Review of Genetic Parameters Estimated at Stallion and Young Horse Performance Tests and Their Correlation with Later Competition Results. Paper read at the 53rd Annual Meeting of the EAAP, 1–4 September, Cairo, Egypt.

» Van Veldhuizen, Arjen. 1995. EPTM evaluation report. KWPN internal report. Harderwijk, the Netherlands.

» Visser-Riedstra, Kathalijne. 2002. Horsonality: a study on the personality of the horse. Ph.D. diss., Wageningen University, the Netherlands. [ISBN 90-6464-178-1. English language dissertation with a Dutch language abstract. Available through www.asg.wur.nl.]

Index

Page numbers in *italic* indicate photographs or illustrations.

Index